Culturally Responsive
Lessons & Activities

Grade 1

All illustrations and photography, including those from Shutterstock.com, are protected by copyright.

Writing: Tiffany Rivera
Monika Davies
Content Editing: Teera Robinson
Lisa Vitarisi Mathews
Copy Editing: Laurie Westrich
Art Direction: Yuki Meyer
Cover Design: Yuki Meyer
Illustration: Mary Rojas
Design/Production: Paula Acojido
Yuki Meyer
Jessica Onken

EMC 8261

Visit
teaching-standards.com
to view a correlation
of this book.
This is a free service.

Correlated to Current Standards

Congratulations on your purchase of some of the finest teaching materials in the world.

Photocopying the pages in this book is permitted for single-classroom use only. Making photocopies for additional classes or schools is prohibited.

For information about other Evan-Moor products, call 1-800-777-4362, fax 1-800-777-4332, or visit our website, www.evan-moor.com.
Entire contents © 2022 Evan-Moor Corporation
18 Lower Ragsdale Drive, Monterey, CA 93940-5746. Printed in USA.

CPSIA: Bradford & Bigelow, Newburyport, MA USA [12/2022]

Contents

Introduction

What's in *Culturally Responsive Lessons and Activities*? 4

How to Use This Book 6

About Culturally Responsive Teaching and Learning 7

Student Contents 8

How Do I Say It? 9

Sharing Forms 10

Units

Nonfiction and Informational Fiction

I Can Do It, Too: Brittney Reese's Story 11

Glad to Be Me: Forrest Goodluck's Story 23

You Can Do a Lot: Jessica Cox's Story 35

Kids Can Help: Moziah Bridges' Story 47

Realistic Fiction

All Families Are Beautiful:
Wendy Learns About Her Family 59

I Like My Culture: Tony Does Like His Mom's Food 71

Do the Right Thing: Friends Do the Right Thing 83

Every Holiday Is Special: Three Holiday Parties 95

Cultural Exploration and Self-Discovery

Classroom Community 107

Culture and Family 119

Classroom Quilt 131

What's in *Culturally Responsive Lessons and Activities*?

8 Nonfiction, Informational Fiction, and Realistic Fiction Units

The units in this book are about people from diverse backgrounds, with different abilities, ethnicities, and origins. Four units feature nonfiction biographical stories or informational fiction stories about people who are inspirational and perseverant. Four units feature realistic fiction stories about authentic situations and challenges that real people experience. Each unit has a different theme and begins with a teacher page that introduces the subject and activities. The story pages and activities are reproducible for students. The unit's theme is shown at the top of each student page.

Examples of themes include:

I Like My Culture

You Can Do a Lot

Every Holiday Is Special

Story

Each of the nonfiction, informational fiction, and realistic fiction units has a reproducible two-page story that the subsequent activities relate to. The story emphasizes the unit's theme.

The stories describe real-life experiences in an age-appropriate way. They tell how people overcame challenges, navigated through complicated situations, and made choices that defined their lives. All of these story subjects and themes were chosen thoughtfully because of their power to inspire and the importance of representation.

Theme-Based Activities

Each unit has an activity that students complete independently, a whole-class or small-group discussion activity, a partner activity, and a project menu. Students choose from hands-on projects, performance projects, and creative writing projects.

Activities in all units vary and are designed to be engaging and open-ended, with a wide variety of response formats. The goal is for students to feel like the activities are providing a "safe space" to share their own unique viewpoints and experiences.

Activities include the following:
- creative writing and drawing
- critical thinking
- games
- visual information
- discussion
- hypothetical scenarios and problem solving
- making choices and justifying opinions
- art projects

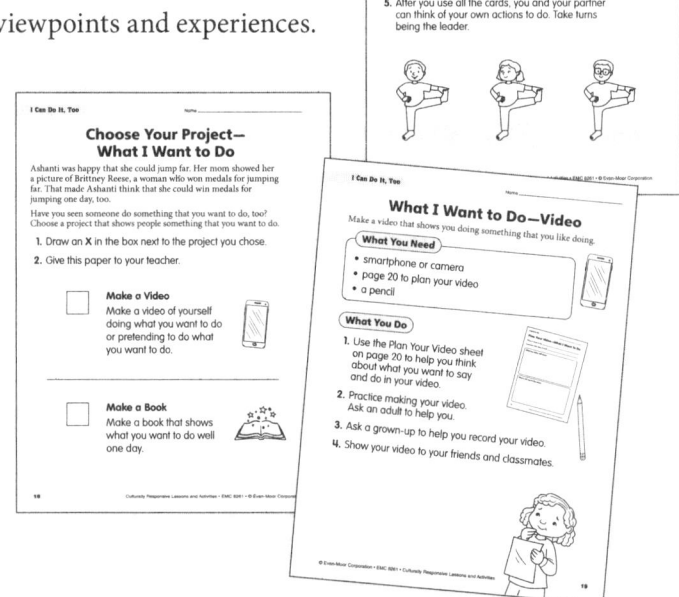

3 Cultural Exploration and Self-Discovery Units

The cultural exploration and self-discovery units are not centered around a text; rather, they feature a variety of engaging and creative activities that invite students to reflect on their own cultures and interactions with the world. The activities prompt students to share their own opinions, tastes, families, and experiences. These activities also support students in being culturally responsive by keeping an open mind, learning about the people around them with the intention of recognizing their value, and considering other viewpoints. Many of the activities provide opportunities for collaboration and whole-class projects. Some collaborative activities include making a class quilt, making handprint art, and playing games.

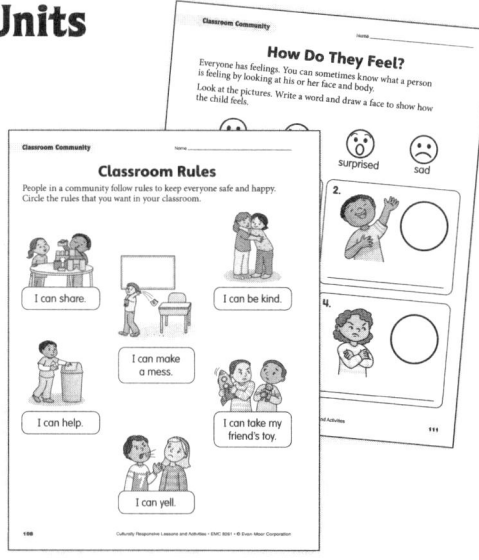

Student Resources

Additional pages provide students with support and provide opportunities for students to take an active role in their learning.

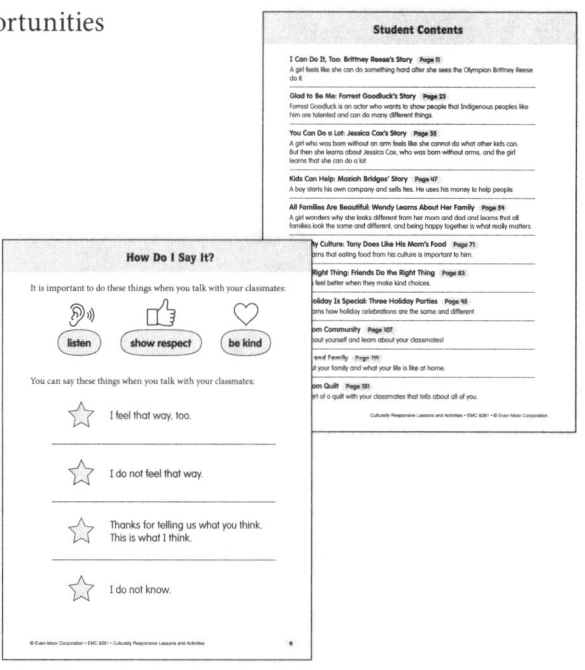

Student Contents

You may wish to allow your students to choose a unit to complete. Reproduce and distribute the Student Contents to students. Review the Student Contents with students. Read aloud the choices of units and descriptions. Have students think about what they are interested in reading, and let the class choose a unit.

How Do I Say It?

You may choose to reproduce and distribute this page to students before you begin the first unit. The text at the top of the page explains the purpose. This page models respectful language that kids may choose to use during a class or group discussion. Read aloud the text and sentences on the page as students follow along silently. Discuss with students what listening, showing respect, and being kind looks and sounds like.

Student and Parent/Guardian Sharing Forms

The Student and Parent/Guardian Sharing Forms are intended to provide a connection between home and school. The purpose is to invite students and their families to communicate directly with the teacher and to take an active role in their learning.

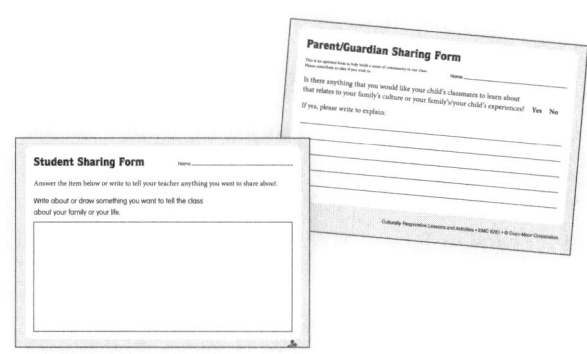

How to Use This Book

Planning Instruction

Nonfiction, Informational Fiction, and Realistic Fiction Units

Teacher Pages

Each unit begins with a teacher page that summarizes the focus of the unit and provides a suggested teaching path.

Nonfiction, Informational Fiction, and Realistic Fiction Stories

These units center around the story and theme, such as Kids Can Help. The story provides context for the activities and projects. You can choose the activities that align with your students' needs or provide opportunities to increase engagement and positive interactions among students. Or you can allow students to choose the theme or person they would like to read about by reproducing the Student Contents on page 8 and distributing it to students.

Independent Activities

Each nonfiction, informational fiction, and realistic fiction story is followed by an independent activity that provides students opportunities to reflect on the story and the theme and relate it to their own lives.

Discussion Activities

Each unit includes a discussion activity. Before the discussion, read the discussion items to students. Have them think about their own opinions and experiences; they may choose to write or draw about them in preparation for the discussion. Before you begin the whole- and small-group discussions, you may wish to reproduce and distribute page 9, How Do I Say It? This page provides ideas and suggestions for statements and sentences that encourage respectful and productive communication.

Partner Activities

Each unit includes partner activities that are intended to help students learn about each other as they also learn more about themselves. To prepare for these activities, consider how you will assign partners or what process you will use to have students choose partners. It is important that students connect with classmates that they may not have in their social circle.

Choose Your Project Activities

Each unit includes a project menu for students to choose from. The project choices include hands-on, performance, and creative writing projects. Many of the projects require materials that are commonly part of classroom art supplies. Before you distribute the Choose Your Project activities to students, you may wish to confirm that you have access to the materials needed.

Cultural Exploration and Self-Discovery Units

Teacher Pages

Each unit begins with a teacher page that summarizes the focus of the unit and provides an overview of the activities and projects in the unit.

Activities, Games, and Projects

These units focus on learning about oneself and others through the lens of culture, family traditions, and people's similarities and differences. The activities, games, and projects range from individual to collaborative and often extend to home and family.

The pages in these units do not have to be completed in sequential order. Choose the activities that you want your students to complete, or offer them the opportunity to choose based on their interests.

About Culturally Responsive Teaching and Learning

Culturally responsive teaching is about connecting students' cultures and life experiences with what they are learning in school. Cultural responsiveness is creating a climate in which all students can feel a sense of belonging while also feeling safe to be their authentic selves as they process the curriculum and academic content.

These are some things you might see in a culturally responsive learning environment:

- Student-choice learning activities
- Students sharing about their home lives, first languages, or other cultural and personal experiences
- A sense of community as an emphasis during learning, in addition to academic content
- Family involvement in the learning process

Evan-Moor's Approach to Culturally Responsive Teaching and Learning

The activities in this book are designed to provide students with choices for how to demonstrate their learning and unique viewpoints. Many of the activities, including the group discussions, give students the opportunity to share about their own families and experiences. Our goal is to help students explore their own individualities, cultures, and life experiences and to help them learn more about their classmates, as well as to help teachers gain insights about who their students are so they can make every student's learning more meaningful. The authentic stories in this book represent people from many backgrounds and reflect the diversity and life experiences of people in our world. We hope these stories are both inspiring and enlightening for students.

Student Contents

I Can Do It, Too: Brittney Reese's Story   Page 11

A girl feels like she can do something hard after she sees the Olympian Brittney Reese do it.

Glad to Be Me: Forrest Goodluck's Story   Page 23

Forrest Goodluck is an actor who wants to show people that Indigenous peoples like him are talented and can do many different things.

You Can Do a Lot: Jessica Cox's Story   Page 35

A girl who was born without an arm feels like she cannot do what other kids can. But then she learns about Jessica Cox, who was born without arms, and the girl learns that she can do a lot.

Kids Can Help: Moziah Bridges' Story   Page 47

A boy starts his own company and sells ties. He uses his money to help people.

All Families Are Beautiful: Wendy Learns About Her Family   Page 59

A girl wonders why she looks different from her mom and dad and learns that all families look the same and different, and being happy together is what really matters.

I Like My Culture: Tony Does Like His Mom's Food   Page 71

A boy learns that eating food from his culture is important to him.

Do the Right Thing: Friends Do the Right Thing   Page 83

Two girls feel better when they make kind choices.

Every Holiday Is Special: Three Holiday Parties   Page 95

A boy learns how holiday celebrations are the same and different.

Classroom Community   Page 107

Share about yourself and learn about your classmates!

Culture and Family   Page 119

Tell about your family and what your life is like at home.

Classroom Quilt   Page 131

Make part of a quilt with your classmates that tells about all of you.

How Do I Say It?

It is important to do these things when you talk with your classmates:

You can say these things when you talk with your classmates:

 I feel that way, too.

_____

 I do not feel that way.

_____

 Thanks for telling us what you think. This is what I think.

_____

 I do not know.

Student Sharing Form

Name _____

Answer the item below or write to tell your teacher anything you want to share about.

Write about or draw something you want to tell the class about your family or your life.

[   ]

- ✂ - - -

Parent/Guardian Sharing Form

This is an optional form to help build a sense of community in our class. Please contribute an idea if you wish to.

Name _____

Is there anything that you would like your child's classmates to learn about that relates to your family's culture or your family's/your child's experiences?   **Yes   No**

If yes, please write to explain:

_____

_____

_____

_____

I Can Do It, Too

Brittney Reese's Story

This unit is about how people can be inspired by other people's accomplishments. Students will read about a young girl who is inspired by Olympic medal long jumper Brittney Reese to believe that she can jump far, too. Students may learn that if other people can do something that seems difficult or out of reach, that maybe they can do it, too. Or students may learn that they can look up to role models and gain inspiration. As you guide students through these topics, consider their varying world views as they share their experiences and make connections to their own lives.

The pages in this unit are reproducible. Reproduce the unit in its entirety or choose the pages that you wish to have your students do. A suggested teaching path is below.

1. **Read the Informational Fiction Story (pages 12 and 13)**
   Distribute one copy of the text to each student. Have students read the text independently or read the text aloud as they follow along silently.

2. **What Do You Want to Do Too? (page 14)**
   Distribute one copy of the page to each student. Guide students in completing the page independently.

3. **Let's Talk About Brittney Reese (page 15)**
   Distribute one copy of the page to each student. Facilitate a whole-group discussion or divide the class into small groups.

   Prepare for discussion:
   Guide students through reading each question. Give them time to think of their answers and to write them if they want to. Then facilitate a group discussion, encouraging students to share their thoughts.

4. **Follow the Leader Partner Activity (pages 16 and 17)**
   Divide students into groups of two. Distribute one copy of each page to each group. Have each group work on the activity together.

5. **Choose Your Project—What I Want to Do (pages 18–22)**
   Distribute one copy of the project menu to each student. Explain to students that they will each choose a project to do. After students have chosen their project, collect the project menus. Reproduce and distribute the following project pages for each student based on the student's choice:

   - Pages 19 and 20 for What I Want to Do—Video
   - Pages 21 and 22 for What I Want to Do—Book

   Decide whether or not students will share their finished projects with the class and instruct students accordingly.

I Can Do It, Too

Ashanti ran into the house. She saw her mom.

"I can jump far!" said Ashanti.

"You can!" said her mom. "I saw you playing outside!"

"I can jump from 1 to 7!" Ashanti said with a big smile.

Ashanti's mom went into her room and came back with a book.

"Look, Ashanti, this is Brittney Reese. She can jump far, too."

Ashanti looked at the picture of Brittney.

"She can jump 7 meters. That's almost 25 feet! She has won many medals for jumping far," said Ashanti's mom.

Ashanti sat down and looked at the pictures in the book.

I Can Do It, Too

Name _____

© Dmitry Rozhkov

"Mom, I'm glad Brittney has won medals for jumping far. I want to try to win medals for jumping far. Now I know that I can do it, too," said Ashanti.

"Sometimes it helps us to see other people do things. It helps us know that maybe we can do those things, too," said Ashanti's mom. "Now, let's go outside and see how far we can jump!"

I Can Do It, Too

Name _____

What Do You Want to Do Too?

When Ashanti saw how far Brittney could jump, it made Ashanti feel like she could do it, too.

Answer the items below.

1. Would you like to do these things, too? Circle **yes** or **no**.

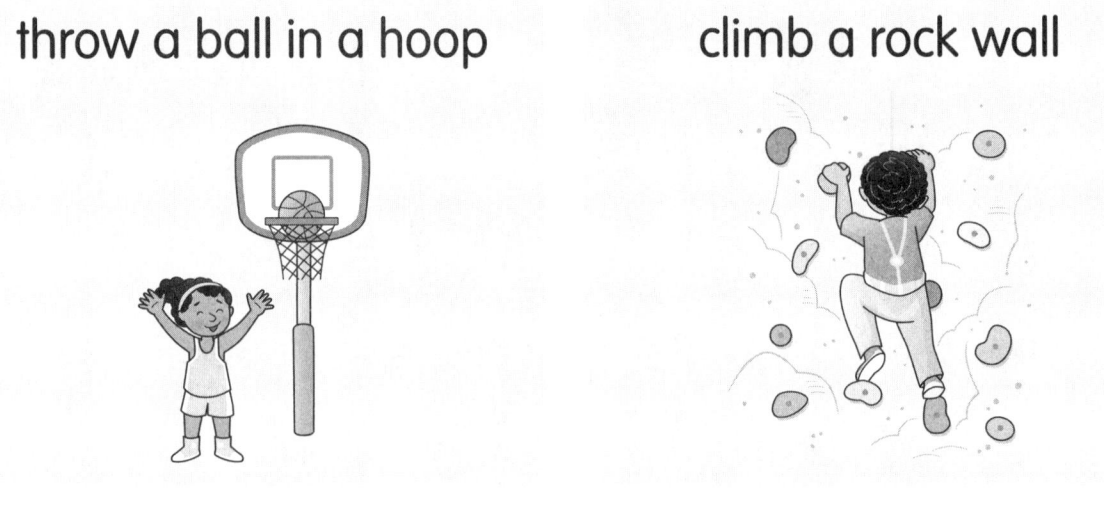

throw a ball in a hoop   climb a rock wall

yes   no   yes   no

2. Draw a picture of something you have seen someone do well that you would like to do, too.

I Can Do It, Too!

I Can Do It, Too

Name _____

Let's Talk About Brittney Reese

Brittney Reese was on the United States Olympic Team. She worked hard and did her best to jump far.

Think about these questions.
Then talk with your classmates.
You can tell them things about you.
You can listen to things about them.

What is something that you work hard to do?

What can you do to try your best?

I Can Do It, Too

Follow the Leader Partner Activity

Sometimes when you see a person doing something, it makes it easier for you to do it. It makes you feel like, "I can do that, too!"

Play a game of follow the leader with your partner. You and your partner take turns being the leader.

1. Cut out the action cards on page 17.

2. Choose an action card. Do the action in front of your partner.

3. Then your partner does the same action.

4. Now it's your partner's turn to be the leader.

5. After you use all the cards, you and your partner can think of your own actions to do. Take turns being the leader.

Follow the Leader Action Cards

I Can Do It, Too

Name _____

Choose Your Project— What I Want to Do

Ashanti was happy that she could jump far. Her mom showed her a picture of Brittney Reese, a woman who won medals for jumping far. That made Ashanti think that she could win medals for jumping one day, too.

Have you seen someone do something that you want to do, too? Choose a project that shows people something that you want to do.

1. Draw an **X** in the box next to the project you chose.
2. Give this paper to your teacher.

☐ **Make a Video**

Make a video of yourself doing what you want to do or pretending to do what you want to do.

☐ **Make a Book**

Make a book that shows what you want to do well one day.

I Can Do It, Too

Name _____

What I Want to Do—Video

Make a video that shows you doing something that you like doing.

What You Need

- smartphone or camera
- page 20 to plan your video
- a pencil

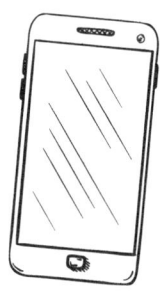

What You Do

1. Use the Plan Your Video sheet on page 20 to help you think about what you want to say and do in your video.

2. Practice making your video. Ask an adult to help you.

3. Ask a grown-up to help you record your video.

4. Show your video to your friends and classmates.

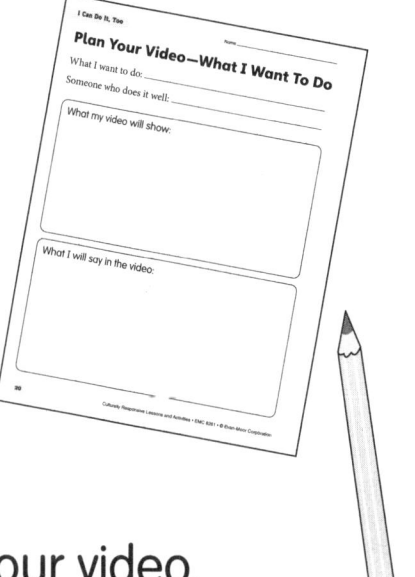

© Evan-Moor Corporation • EMC 8261 • Culturally Responsive Lessons and Activities

I Can Do It, Too

Name _____

Plan Your Video—What I Want To Do

What I want to do: _____

Someone who does it well: _____

What my video will show:

What I will say in the video:

What I Want to Do—Book

Make a book that shows and tells what you want to do.
If you saw someone do it well, write about that person, too.

What You Need

- 2 sheets of white paper
- page 22
- a stapler
- a pencil
- scissors
- crayons or markers

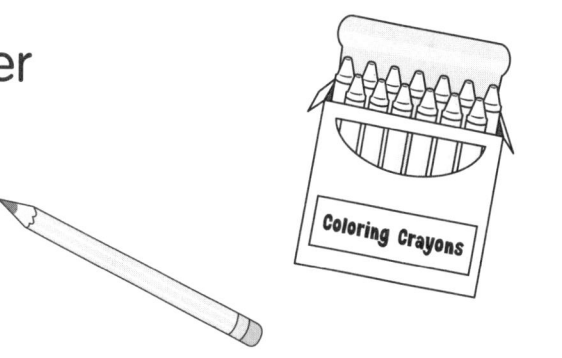

What You Do

1. Cut out and fold the paper on page 22 to make a cover for the book. Then fold two sheets of paper and put them in the middle of the cover to make a book. Staple the book together.

2. Write a title for your book on the front cover. Draw a picture on it.

3. Draw pictures and write words or sentences on the inside pages. Tell and show what you want to do one day. If you saw someone do it well, write and draw about that person, too.

4. Show your book to someone.

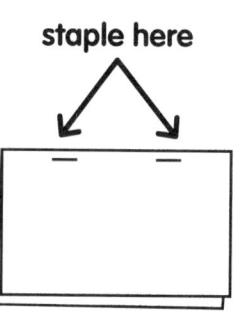
staple here

I Can Do It, Too

———————————————————— fold ————————————————————

I Can Do It, Too

Glad to Be Me

Forrest Goodluck's Story

This unit is about representation, stereotypes, and being proud of who you are. It features Forrest Goodluck, an Indigenous American actor who is proud of his heritage. He is proud to represent Indigenous American peoples in movies. Students may have had their own experiences with stereotypes, or they may learn about them. As you guide students through these topics, consider their varying world views as they share their experiences and make connections to their own lives.

The pages in this unit are reproducible. Reproduce the unit in its entirety or choose the pages that you wish to have your students do. A suggested teaching path is below.

1. **Read the Nonfiction Story (pages 24 and 25)**
   Distribute one copy of the text to each student. Have students read the text independently or read the text aloud as they follow along silently.

2. **Why I Am Proud (page 26)**
   Distribute one copy of the page to each student. Guide students in completing the page independently.

3. **Let's Talk About Forrest Goodluck (page 27)**
   Distribute one copy of the page to each student. Facilitate a whole-group discussion or divide the class into small groups.

   Prepare for discussion:
   Guide students through reading each question. Give them time to think of their answers and to write them if they want to. Then facilitate a group discussion, encouraging students to share their thoughts.

4. **Glad to Be Me Partner Activity (pages 28 and 29)**
   Before you distribute the activity to students, you may wish to confirm that you have access to the materials needed. Divide students into groups of two. Distribute one copy of each page to each group. Have each group work on the activity together.

5. **Choose Your Project—Proud of Who I Am (pages 30–34)**
   Distribute one copy of the project menu to each student. Explain to students that they will each choose a project to do. After students have chosen their project, collect the project menus. Reproduce and distribute the following project pages for each student based on the student's choice:

   - Pages 31 and 32 for Proud of Who I Am—Handprint Picture
   - Pages 33 and 34 for Proud of Who I Am—Finish the Story

   Decide whether or not students will share their finished projects with the class and instruct students accordingly.

Forrest Goodluck's Story

© Kathy Hutchins / Shutterstock.com

Forrest Goodluck was born in 1998. He is an American actor.

He is famous for acting in TV shows and movies. He works with other famous actors, too.

Forrest is proud of the work that he does. He is also proud of himself. Forrest is an Indigenous American who is from many different tribes. He is glad to be who he is.

Forrest started acting when he was in 5th grade. He acted at his school. He loved it! His pet dog was in his first play, too.

Forrest believes that acting is a way to tell stories. Forrest likes to tell stories about Indigenous peoples.

Forrest plays characters who do different things. In one movie, his character plays hockey. In another story, his job is finding animals in the wild.

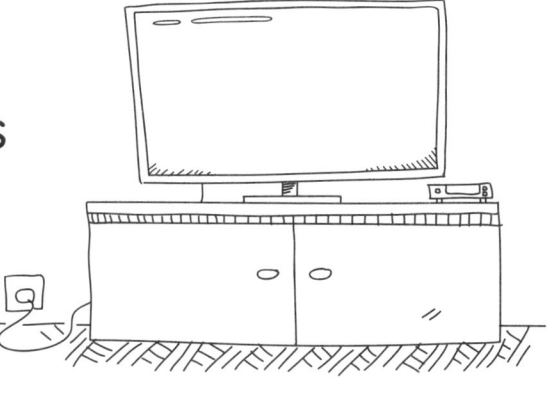

In the past, many TV shows and movies showed Indigenous peoples as being nearly the same as each other. Forrest likes to be in movies that show how Indigenous people are different from each other. In the real world, all people are different.

Forrest wants people to learn about Indigenous American culture when they see him in movies. He also wants people to know that Indigenous Americans are not all the same. They do not all dress the same and do the same things. They are all different. He is helping people know that. That's one reason why he is so proud of his work and his culture.

Glad to Be Me

Name _____

Why I Am Proud

Forrest Goodluck is proud to be an Indigenous American. He is glad to be who he is. What makes you glad to be you?

Answer the items below.

1. Do these things make you glad to be you?
Circle **yes** or **no**.

my culture	things I can do	how I treat other people
yes no	yes no	yes no

2. Draw a picture of something that makes you proud to be you.

Let's Talk About Forrest Goodluck

Forrest Goodluck is glad to be from different tribes. He is also proud of the work he does.

Think about these questions.
Then talk with your classmates.
You can tell them about you.
You can listen to learn about them.

What makes you glad to be who you are?

Do you think it is important to like who you are?

Glad to Be Me Partner Activity

There are lots of things that can make people feel glad to be who they are. You will use the sentences below to make bookmarks that remind you why you are glad to be you!

1. Cut out the sentence cards.

2. With your partner, read each sentence card.

3. Take turns picking a card to glue to your bookmark. You will each get three cards.

I am glad to be me because I am kind.

I am glad to be me because I am smart.

I am glad to be me because I am a good friend.

I am glad to be me because I help people.

I am glad to be me because I love my family.

I am glad to be me because I like to have fun.

Glad to Be Me

Cut out the bookmarks.
Each partner gets one.
Glue your sentence cards to your bookmark.
Then color your bookmark.

I am glad to be me	I am glad to be me
glue	glue
glue	glue
glue	glue

Glad to Be Me

Glad to Be Me

Name _____

Choose Your Project— Proud of Who I Am

Forrest Goodluck is proud of who he is. He is glad that he is an Indigenous American. He is glad to do the work he does.

Think about what makes you like yourself. Choose a project that shows why you are glad to be you.

1. Draw an **X** in the box next to the project you chose.
2. Give this paper to your teacher.

☐ **Make a Handprint Picture**

Make a handprint picture. Then decorate it with pictures and words to show that you are proud to be you.

☐ **Finish the Story**

Finish the story to tell why you are proud to be you.

Proud of Who I Am—Handprint Picture

Make a handprint. Decorate it with words and pictures to show why you like being you!

What You Need

- a sheet of construction paper
- words on page 32
- paint
- a paper plate
- crayons or markers
- scissors
- glue or tape

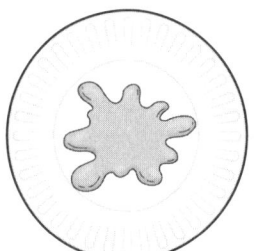

What You Do

1. Put paint on a paper plate.
2. Press one hand onto the paint. Then press the same hand onto the paper.
3. Let the paint handprint dry.
4. After the paint dries, draw pictures and write or glue words around your handprint. You can cut out the words on page 32 if you want to.
5. Hang your picture where you can see it.

Glad to Be Me

I am proud of who I am!	helpful
smart	kind
happy	fun
loved	I work hard

Glad to Be Me

Proud of Who I Am—Finish the Story

Write words to finish a story that tells why you are proud to be you.

What You Need

- a sheet of colored construction paper
- page 34
- a pencil
- crayons or markers
- glue or tape

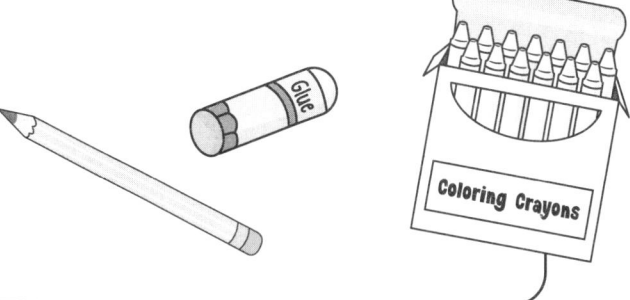

What You Do

1. On page 34, write about yourself to finish the story.

2. Then color the pictures. You can draw your own pictures, too.

3. Glue your story to the construction paper.

4. Hang it where you can see it.

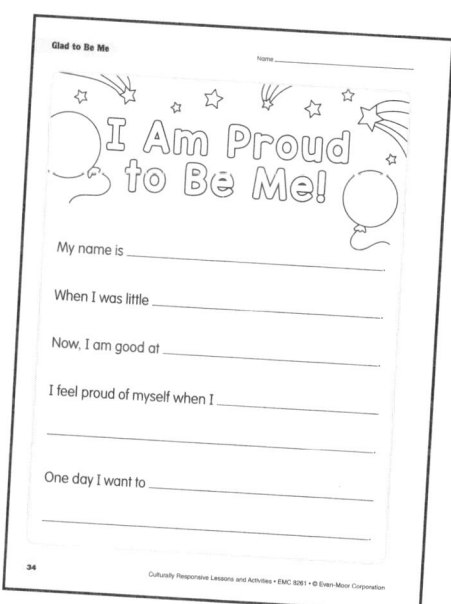

Glad to Be Me

My name is _____.

When I was little, _____.

Now, I am good at _____.

I feel proud of myself when I _____
_____.

One day I want to _____
_____.

You Can Do a Lot

Jessica Cox's Story

This unit emphasizes how every person has the ability to achieve a lot, although all people face unique challenges or situations. Students will read a story that features Jessica Cox, a licensed pilot and black belt in Taekwondo who was born without arms. Jessica inspires people because she is an accomplished woman. Students may have challenges or disabilities that affect their own lives, or they may learn for the first time that people with disabilities can choose to not let their disabilities stop them from accomplishing their dreams. As you guide students through these topics, consider their varying world views as they share their experiences and make connections to their own lives.

The pages in this unit are reproducible. Reproduce the unit in its entirety or choose the pages that you wish to have your students do. A suggested teaching path is below.

1. **Read the Informational Fiction Story (pages 36 and 37)**
   Distribute one copy of the text to each student. Have students read the text independently or read the text aloud as they follow along silently.

2. **You Can Do a Lot (page 38)**
   Distribute one copy of the page to each student. Guide students in completing the page independently.

3. **Let's Talk About Jessica Cox (page 39)**
   Distribute one copy of the page to each student. Facilitate a whole-group discussion or divide the class into small groups.

   Prepare for discussion:
   Guide students through reading each question. Give them time to think of their answers and to write them if they want to. Then facilitate a group discussion, encouraging students to share their thoughts.

4. **All People Can Do a Lot Partner Activity (pages 40 and 41)**
   Divide students into groups of two. Distribute one copy of each page to each group. Have each group work on the activities together.

5. **Choose Your Project—I Can Do a Lot (pages 42–46)**
   Distribute one copy of the project menu to each student. Explain to students that they will each choose a project to do. After students have chosen their project, collect the project menus. Reproduce and distribute the following project pages for each student based on the student's choice:

   - Pages 43 and 44 for I Can Do a Lot—Picture Frame
   - Pages 45 and 46 for I Can Do a Lot—Poster

   Decide whether or not students will share their finished projects with the class and instruct students accordingly.

Jessica's Cox's Story

Shyla came home from school. She looked sad. Her dad saw her.

"Shyla, you look sad," he said. "What is wrong?"

"I could not play on the bars at school," Shyla said. "My friend said it is because I only have one arm."

Shyla was born with only one arm. She used her right arm to write and draw. Shyla did not have a left arm. She used her right arm to do everything.

Her dad hugged Shyla. Then he showed her a picture.

Shyla looked at the picture. She saw a woman smiling. The woman did not have arms.

"This is Jessica Cox," Shyla's dad said. "She is cool! She can do a lot of things." He showed Shyla more pictures.

"Dad, why is Jessica in a plane?" Shyla asked.

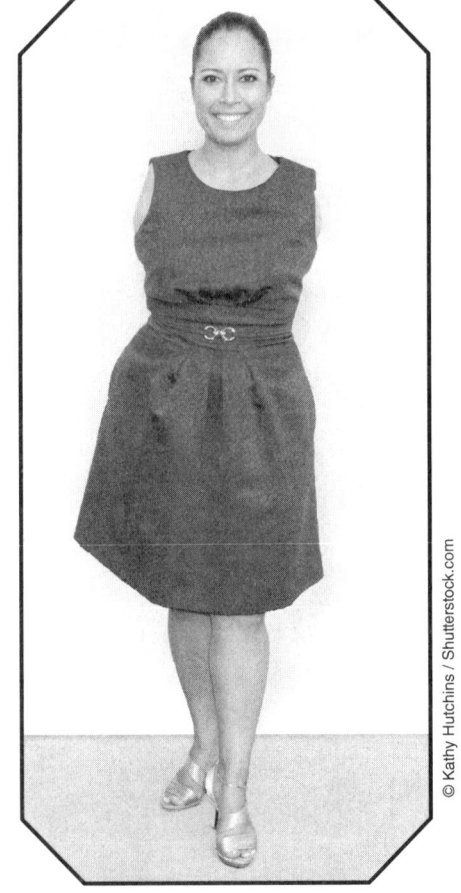

Jessica Cox

"She is a pilot," her dad said.

"Cool!" said Shyla.

They saw more pictures. There was a picture of Jessica in white clothes with a black belt. Jessica was doing Taekwondo! She looked strong. There were also pictures of Jessica driving a car and playing piano.

Jessica Cox doing Taekwondo

"Wow, Jessica can do a lot," Shyla said.

"You can do a lot, too, Shyla!" said her dad. "Everyone's body is different. No person can do everything. But we can all do a lot."

Shyla looked at her body. She thought of what she could do. She could write her name. She could dance to music. She could help her mom bake cookies. She could run fast. She could read books. She could do a lot, too! She was like Jessica.

You Can Do a Lot

Jessica can do a lot. So can Shyla! Shyla can write and draw. She can help bake cookies. She can run fast.

Answer the items below.

1. Can you do these things? Circle **yes** or **no**.

run fast	paint a picture	listen to others
yes no	yes no	yes no

2. Draw a picture of something you can do.

I can do a lot! This is something I can do.

Let's Talk About Jessica Cox

Jessica Cox was born without arms, and she can do a lot of different things.

Think about these questions.
Then talk with your classmates.
You can tell them how you feel.
You can listen to how they feel.

What is something that you work hard to do?

What can you do to try your best?

You Can Do a Lot

All People Can Do a Lot Partner Activity

Cut the page in half. Give each partner a half. Each partner cuts out the pictures. You will use them to do page 41.

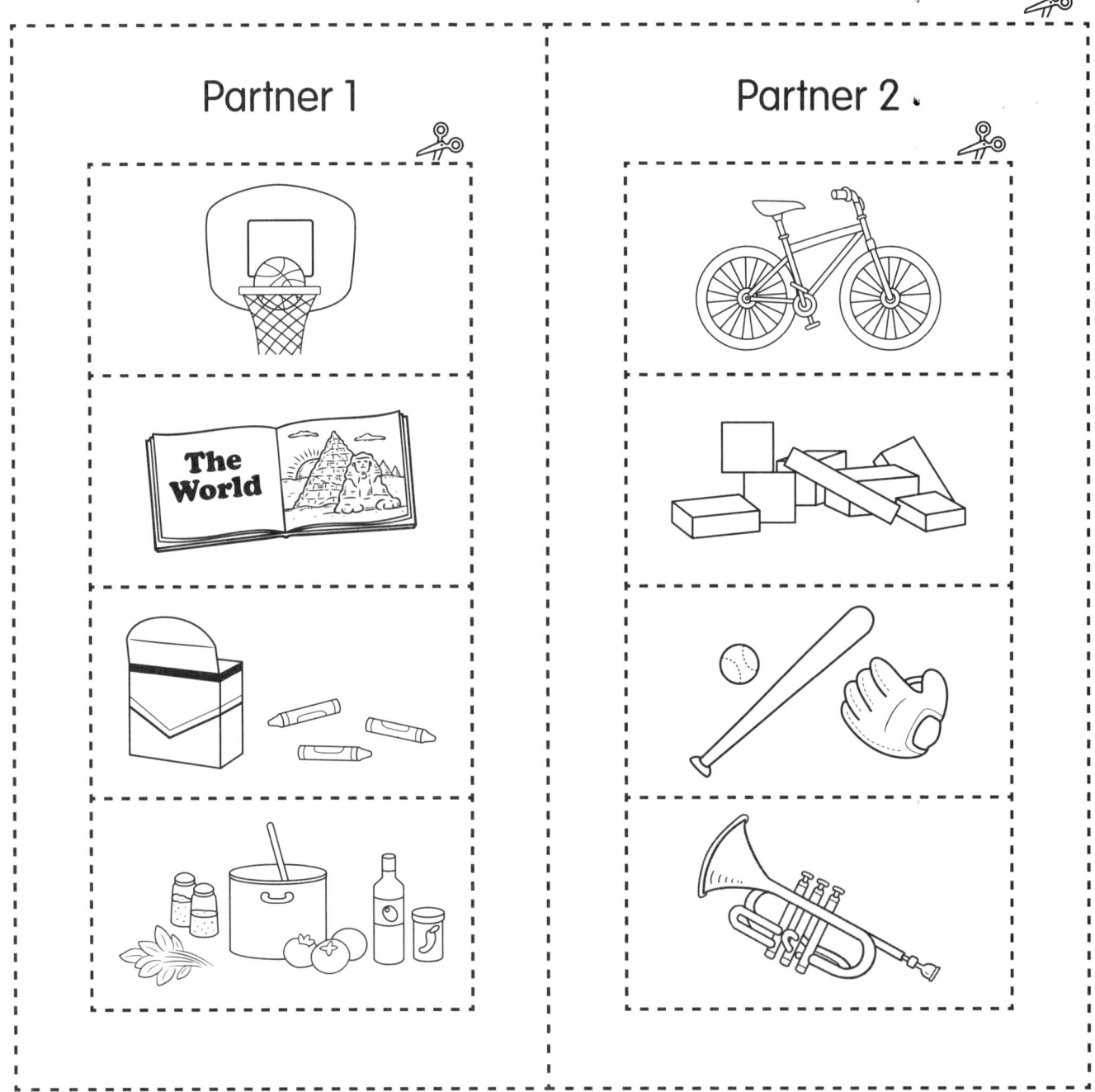

You Can Do a Lot

Name _____

Name _____

All People Can Do a Lot Partner Activity

You learned that every person's body is different, and every person has things he or she can do.

Read each sentence. Look at the pictures you cut out. Each partner can pick one picture that shows what that person can do. Glue it in the box.

Mike cannot hear. He can do a lot.

| glue | glue |

Sara cannot walk. She can do a lot.

| glue | glue |

Tim has one arm. He can do a lot.

| glue | glue |

Choose Your Project—
I Can Do a Lot

Jessica can drive a car. She can fly a plane. She can play the piano. Jessica can do a lot!

You can do a lot, too. What are some things you can do? Choose a project to show some of the things you can do.

1. Draw an **X** in the box next to the project you chose.
2. Give this paper to your teacher.

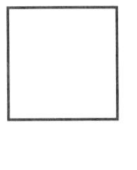 **Make a Picture Frame**
Make a frame for a picture that shows what you can do!

 **Make a Poster**
Make a poster that tells and shows some of the things you can do.

I Can Do a Lot—Picture Frame

Make a picture and a frame that shows something you can do.

What You Need

- a large sheet of construction paper
- page 44
- crayons or markers
- a smartphone or light-colored paper that is smaller than the sheet of construction paper
- scissors
- glue or tape

What You Do

1. Ask someone to take a picture of you doing something that you like to do. Or you can draw a picture on the light-colored paper.

2. Glue or tape the picture onto the construction paper.

3. Color and cut out the frame parts on page 44.

4. Glue or tape the frame parts onto the construction paper in the correct place: top, bottom, left, and right.

5. Now you have a framed picture that shows what you can do!

You Can Do a Lot

left   **right**   **top**   **bottom**

I Can Do a Lot—Poster

Make a poster with words and pictures to show what you can do.

What You Need

- a large sheet of construction paper
- page 46
- crayons or markers
- a pencil
- glue
- scissors
- things to decorate a poster, such as dried pasta, beads, buttons, cotton balls, paint, glitter, pompoms, dried leaves, foil, etc.

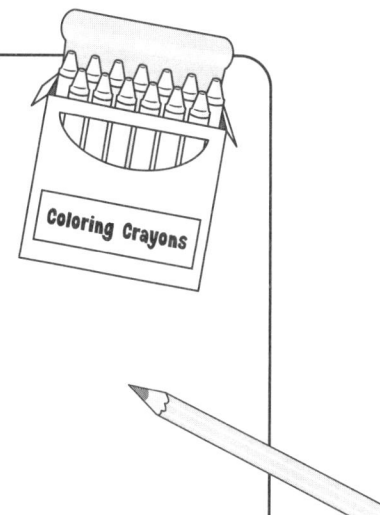

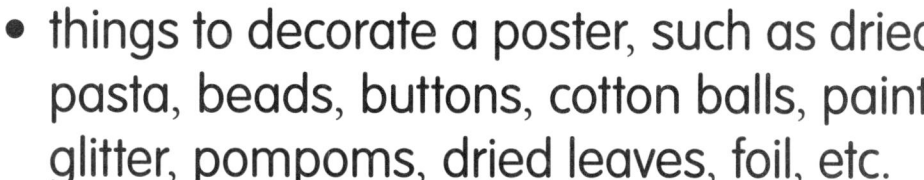

What You Do

1. You can draw your own pictures for your poster. Or you can cut out and color the pictures on page 46 and glue them to your poster.

2. Write your own words to tell about some things you can do.

3. Add decorations to your poster.

4. Show your poster to your friends.

You Can Do a Lot

Kids Can Help

Moziah Bridges' Story

This unit is about how kids can help people and how you're never too young to help. Students will read a story that features Moziah Bridges, a boy who started his own business designing and selling bow ties. Moziah uses the money he earns to help people in his community. Students may have had their own experiences with helping people, or they may learn how even young kids can make a big difference in the world. As you guide students through these topics, consider their varying world views as they share their experiences and make connections to their own lives.

The pages in this unit are reproducible. Reproduce the unit in its entirety or choose the pages that you wish to have your students do. A suggested teaching path is below.

1. **Read the Informational Fiction Story (pages 48 and 49)**
   Distribute one copy of the text to each student. Have students read the text independently or read the text aloud as they follow along silently.

2. **I Can Help (page 50)**
   Distribute one copy of the page to each student. Guide students in completing the page independently.

3. **Let's Talk About Moziah Bridges (page 51)**
   Distribute one copy of the page to each student. Facilitate a whole-group discussion or divide the class into small groups.

   Prepare for discussion:
   Guide students through reading each question. Give them time to think of their answers and to write them if they want to. Then facilitate a group discussion, encouraging students to share their thoughts.

4. **Match to Help and Helping Hands Partner Activities (pages 52 and 53)**
   Divide students into groups of two. Distribute one copy of each page to each student. Have each group work on the activities together.

5. **Choose Your Project—How I Can Help (pages 54–58)**
   Distribute one copy of the project menu to each student. Explain to students that they will each choose a project to do. After students have chosen their project, collect the project menus. Reproduce and distribute the following project pages for each student based on the student's choice:

   - Pages 55 and 56 for How I Can Help—Video
   - Pages 57 and 58 for How I Can Help—Poster

   Decide whether or not students will share their finished projects with the class and instruct students accordingly.

I Can Help Other People

Kenny and his dad washed his mom's car. Then they went to play at the park.

Kenny saw a girl playing by herself. She looked sad. She was wearing old shoes that had big holes in them.

"Hi," Kenny said to the girl. "I'm Kenny. Do you want to play?"

Kenny and the girl played on the swings. The girl told Kenny that she felt sad sometimes because she was hungry. Kenny felt sad for her.

On the way home from the park, Kenny told his dad about the girl. "Dad, that girl was hungry. And she had holes in her shoes. I wish I could help her. But kids like me can't help."

Kenny's dad said, "Look at the tie I have on, Kenny. Do you know who made it?"

Kenny looked at the tie and shook his head.

"A kid named Moziah Bridges made this tie," said Dad. "He started making ties when he was only 9 years old."

"No way! A kid made that?" asked Kenny.

Kids Can Help

Kenny's dad laughed. "Yes, kids can do anything!" he said. "Moziah sells his ties all around the world. He uses the money he makes to help other kids."

"How does he help?" asked Kenny.

"Some families do not have money to buy food or clothes," said Kenny's dad. "He also helps pay for kids to go to summer camp."

© WENN Rights Ltd / Alamy Stock Photo

"Wow, if Moziah can help, I think I can help people, too!" said Kenny. "I have shoes that are too small for me. I can give them to people who need them, like the girl at the park!"

"That is a great idea!" said Kenny's dad.

"I think we should wash people's cars, too!" said Kenny. "We can get even more money. Then we can use it to buy food for people."

"Kenny, it sounds like you will help a lot of people, just like Moziah," said Dad.

Kids Can Help

Name _____

I Can Help

You can help people in many ways.

1. Draw a picture of one way you help your family or friends.

2. Would you like to do these things to help?
Circle **yes** or **no**.

pick up my toys   sweep the floor

yes   no   yes   no

3. Finish the sentence. Tell how you feel when you help.

I feel _____ when I help people.

Kids Can Help

Name _____

Let's Talk About Moziah Bridges

Moziah Bridges is a kid who makes and sells ties. He uses some of the money he makes to help people.

Think about these questions. Then talk with your classmates. You can tell them what you think. You can listen to what they think.

Do you think it is a good idea for Moziah to use some of his money to send kids to summer camp? Tell why or why not.

If you made money from selling things, would you use some of it to help people? Tell why or why not.

Kids Can Help

Name _____

Match to Help Partner Activity

Everyone needs help sometimes.

Look at the pictures with your partner. Then draw a line to give each child what he or she needs. Last, show your partner your answers.

Kids Can Help

Name _____

Helping Hands Partner Activity

You can help other people. Inside one hand, draw a picture of one way you can help a friend. Then write about it on the other hand. Last, show your Helping Hands to your partner.

Kids Can Help

Name _____

Choose Your Project— How I Can Help

Moziah Bridges made money from selling bow ties. He used some of the money to help kids go to summer camp. You can help kids, too.

Choose a project that shows what you would like to sell or do to make money and help people.

1. Draw an **X** in the box next to the project you chose.
2. Give this paper to your teacher.

☐ **Make a Video**
Make a video that shows something you can sell or do to make money to help other people.

☐ **Make a Poster**
Make a poster with pictures that shows what you could sell or do to help other people.

Culturally Responsive Lessons and Activities • EMC 8261 • © Evan-Moor Corporation

Kids Can Help

Name _____

How I Can Help—Video

Make a video that tells and shows what you could sell or do to make money. Tell how you could use the money to help others.

What You Need

- a smartphone or other device that can record video
- page 56 to plan your video
- a pencil

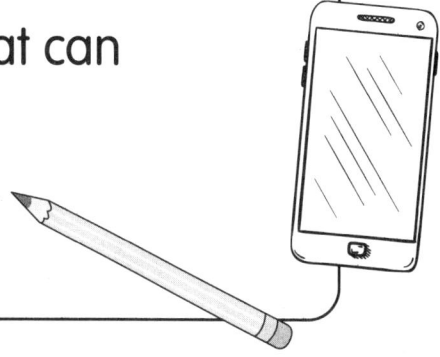

What You Do

1. Use the Plan Your Video sheet on page 56 to help you think about what you want to say and do in your video.

2. Practice making your video. Have a grown-up help you.

3. Have a grown-up help you record your video. Then show it to your friends and classmates.

Kids Can Help — Name _____

Plan Your Video

This is what I will sell or do to make money: _____
_____

This is how I will help kids in my town: _____
_____

What my video will show:

What I will say:

Kids Can Help   Name _____

How I Can Help—Poster

Make a poster with words and pictures to show what you would sell or do to make money and help other people.

What You Need

- a large sheet of construction paper
- page 58
- crayons or markers
- glue
- scissors
- things to decorate a poster, such as dried pasta, beads, buttons, cotton balls, paint, glitter, pompoms, dried leaves, foil, etc.

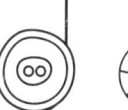

What You Do

1. You can draw your own pictures for your poster. Or you can cut out and color the pictures on page 58 and glue them to your poster.

2. Write your own words to tell what you will sell or do. Tell how you will help other people.

3. Add decorations to your poster.

4. Show your poster to your friends.

All Families Are Beautiful

Wendy Learns About Her Family

This unit is about how all families are beautiful due to their uniqueness and that it is natural to be curious about our own backgrounds. Students will read about Wendy, a girl who has family members from different countries. She wonders why some people in her family look different from one another and learns a little more about her family's background. Students might have a family with individuals who look different from each other, so they might connect to the story, or they might learn how there are many kinds of families. As you guide students through these topics, consider their varying world views as they share their experiences and make connections to their own lives.

The pages in this unit are reproducible. Reproduce the unit in its entirety or choose the pages that you wish to have your students do. A suggested teaching path is below.

1. **Read the Realistic Fiction Story (pages 60 and 61)**
   Distribute one copy of the text to each student. Have students read the text independently or read the text aloud as they follow along silently.

2. **Me and My Family (page 62)**
   Distribute one copy of the page to each student. Guide students in completing the page independently.

3. **Let's Talk About the Story (page 63)**
   Distribute one copy of the page to each student. Facilitate a whole-group discussion or divide the class into small groups.

   Prepare for discussion:
   Guide students through reading each item. Give them time to think of their answers and to write them if they want to. Then facilitate a group discussion, encouraging students to share their thoughts.

4. **Family Pictures and Meet My Family Partner Activities (pages 64 and 65)**
   Divide students into groups of two. Distribute one copy of page 64 to each student. Distribute one copy of page 65 to each group. Have each group work on the activities together.

5. **Choose Your Project—My Family Is Beautiful (pages 66–70)**
   Distribute one copy of the project menu to each student. Explain to students that they will each choose a project to do. After students have chosen their project, collect the project menus. Reproduce and distribute the following project pages for each student based on the student's choice:
   - Pages 67 and 68 for My Family Is Beautiful—Painting
   - Pages 69 and 70 for My Family Is Beautiful—Family Tree

   Decide whether or not students will share their finished projects with the class and instruct students accordingly.

Wendy Learns About Her Family

"I look different from you," Wendy says to her mom. She and her mom are sitting on the sofa. They are looking at pictures of their family. Some of the pictures are really old.

Wendy's mom looks at a picture. She nods her head. "Yes, I look a little different from you. We also look a little bit the same."

"But I want to look just like you," Wendy says. She frowns. "I don't know why I look so different from you."

Wendy's mom smiles. She says, "It's good that we look a bit different. If you look like me, then how will I know who you are?" Mom laughs. Wendy smiles. "I love you because you are you," Mom says.

Wendy looks at more pictures. She points to her granny. "We all look different," says Wendy.

"Yes," says her mom. "That is because our family comes from different places."

All Families Are Beautiful

"Where is Dad from?" asks Wendy. "Why does he have such a big beard? And why is his beard red?"

Wendy's mom laughs again. "Your dad is from America. His dad is from Ireland, and that is another place."

"Where are you from?" Wendy asks.

"I grew up in China," says her mom. "My parents are Chinese."

"So I don't look like you because you are from a different place?" Wendy asks. "Do people everywhere look different?"

"Sometimes, but not always," said Wendy's mom. She hugs Wendy. "And you do look like me a little. Your hair is the same color as mine. You also look a little like your dad. You look the same as both of us, but also different."

"Is it okay that we all look different?" Wendy asks.

"Yes, it is wonderful," says her mom. "We are all different people. So we should all look different."

Wendy looks at the family picture again. Everyone has big smiles on their faces. "Well, we all look so happy!" she says. "That's one way we all look the same!"

All Families Are Beautiful

Name _____

Me and My Family

Wendy has 3 people in her family. One person in her family is her mom. Another person is her dad.

Tell about you and your family. Then draw a picture of your family.

1. There are _____ people in my family.
   write how many

2. Do you like to do these things with your family? Circle **yes** or **no**.

   eat new foods play games

   yes   **no** **yes**   **no**

3. This is my family.

   ┌─────────────────────────────────────┐
   │   │
   │   │
   │   │
   │   │
   │   │
   └─────────────────────────────────────┘

All Families Are Beautiful

Let's Talk About the Story

Wendy learned more about her family. A lot of families have people who look different from each other. All families are different than other families.

Think about these items.
Then talk with your classmates.
You can tell what you think.
You can listen to what they think.

Why do you think Wendy wanted to look like her mom?

Think about reasons why you love your family.

All Families Are Beautiful

Name _____

Family Pictures Partner Activity

Every family is different from other families in some ways. That's what makes every family special.

Read the words. Look at the pictures. Then draw a line to match the words to the pictures. Last, show your answers to your partner.

I like that my big sister and I have different hair. •

•

I like that I am the only kid in my family. •

•

I like that I have lots of brothers and sisters! •

•

Culturally Responsive Lessons and Activities • EMC 8261 • © Evan-Moor Corporation

All Families Are Beautiful

Meet My Family Partner Activity

Families are different and beautiful. Draw to show one way your family is beautiful. Cut out your picture and give it to your partner.

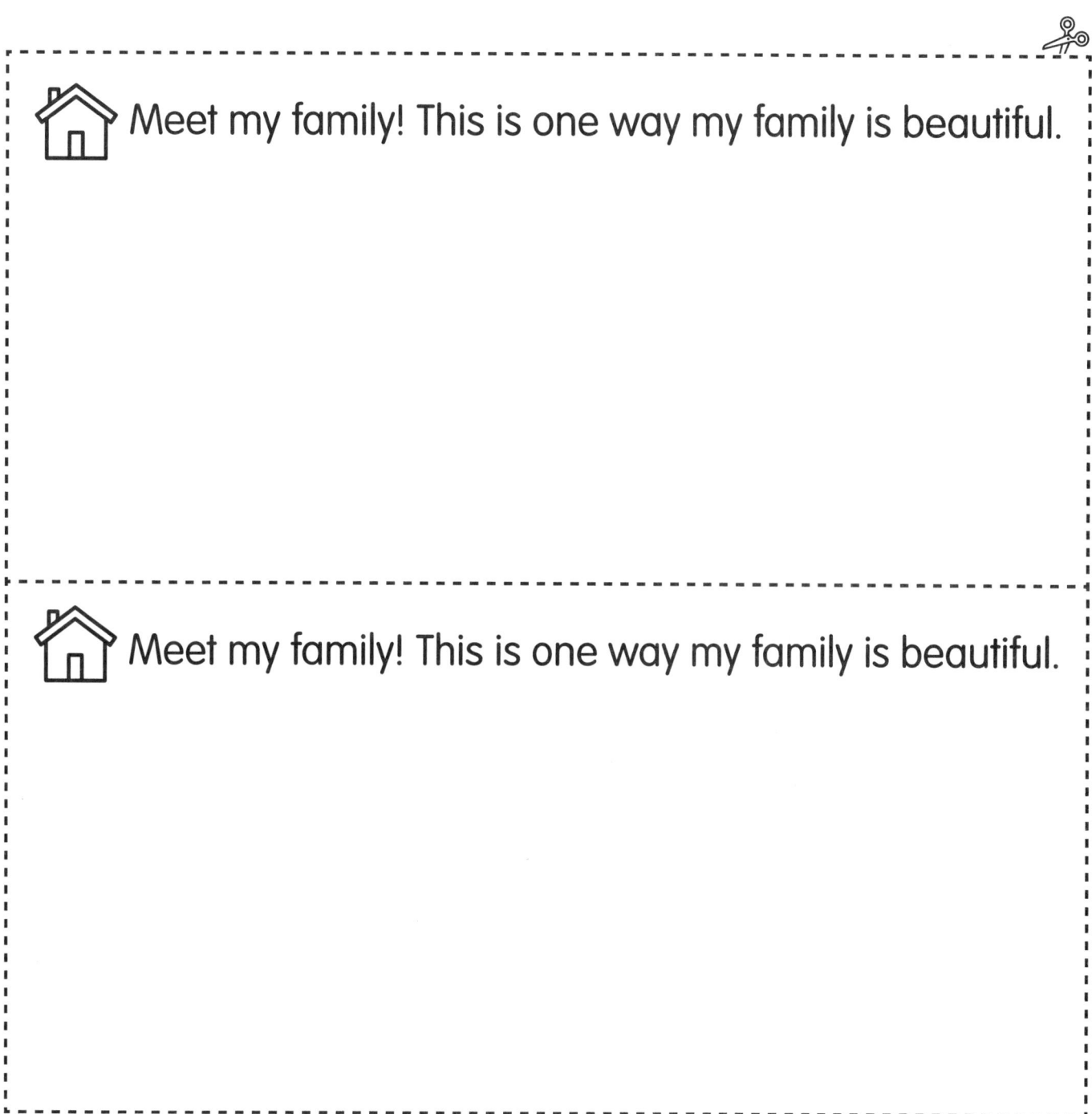

All Families Are Beautiful

All Families Are Beautiful

Name _____

Choose Your Project— My Family Is Beautiful

Wendy's family comes from different places. Her mom came from China. Her dad came from America and Ireland. Everyone in their family looks a little different. Wendy's family is beautiful.

Your family is beautiful, too. Choose a project that shows you with your beautiful family.

1. Draw an **X** in the box next to the project you chose.
2. Give this paper to your teacher.

☐ **Paint a Picture**
Paint a picture that shows you and your beautiful family.

☐ **Make a Family Tree**
Make a family tree that shows pictures of your family.

All Families Are Beautiful

Name _____

My Family Is Beautiful—Painting

Paint a picture of you with your beautiful family.

What You Need

- a large sheet of construction paper
- page 68
- paints
- a paintbrush
- scissors
- glue

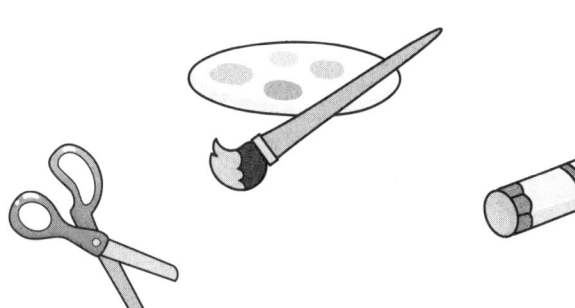

What You Do

1. You can paint your own picture to show how your family is beautiful, or you can paint the pictures on page 68.

2. If you use the pictures on page 68, first cut them out. Then glue them to your construction paper. Last, paint them.

3. Let your painting dry.

4. Show your painting to your friends.

 All Families Are Beautiful

Name _____

My Family Is Beautiful— Family Tree

Make a family tree that shows pictures of your family.

What You Need

- photographs of you and your family that you can cut out or cut around
- page 70
- scissors
- crayons
- glue or tape
- pen or marker
- a sheet of construction paper
- materials to decorate around the tree, such as glitter, dried pasta, cotton balls, colored tissue paper, beads, buttons, foil, etc.

What You Do

1. Ask an adult to help you find pictures of you and your family that you can cut out. Or you can draw pictures of you and your family and cut them out.

2. Cut out the tree on page 70. Then glue it onto the construction paper.

3. Glue or tape pictures of you and your family onto the tree. Cut the pictures to make them smaller if you want to.

4. Write names for everyone on your family tree.

5. Decorate the construction paper around the family tree.

© Evan-Moor Corporation • EMC 8261 • Culturally Responsive Lessons and Activities

I Like My Culture

Tony Does Like His Mom's Food

This unit is about learning to accept ourselves and the cultures that help shape who we are. It's about appreciating cultural traditions. Students will read about Tony, a young Filipino boy who gets tired of eating Filipino food every night with his family. He starts eating different food, but soon discovers he misses eating food from his culture with his family. Students may have experiences with struggling to like certain parts of their own culture, so they might connect to the story. Or they may learn how there are special parts to every culture. As you guide students through these topics, consider their varying world views as they share their experiences and make connections to their own lives.

The pages in this unit are reproducible. Reproduce the unit in its entirety or choose the pages that you wish to have your students do. A suggested teaching path is below.

1. **Read the Realistic Fiction Story (pages 72 and 73)**
   Distribute one copy of the text to each student. Have students read the text independently or read the text aloud as they follow along silently.

2. **My Culture's Food (page 74)**
   Distribute one copy of the page to each student. Guide students in completing the page independently.

3. **Let's Talk About the Story (page 75)**
   Distribute one copy of the page to each student. Facilitate a whole-group discussion or divide the class into small groups.

   Prepare for discussion:
   Guide students through reading each question. Give them time to think of their answers and to write them if they want to. Then facilitate a group discussion, encouraging students to share their thoughts.

4. **Let's Make Dinner! Partner Activity (pages 76 and 77)**
   Divide students into groups of two. Distribute one copy of each page to each group. Have each group work on the activity together.

5. **Choose Your Project Menu—Be Yourself (pages 78–82)**
   Distribute one copy of the project menu to each student. Explain to students that they will each choose a project to do. After students have chosen their project, collect the project menus. Reproduce and distribute the following project pages for each student based on the student's choice:

   - Pages 79 and 80 for I Like My Culture—Painting
   - Pages 81 and 82 for I Like My Culture—Video

   Decide whether or not students will share their finished projects with the class and instruct students accordingly.

Tony Does Like His Mom's Food

It was time to eat. Tony looked at his plate. His mom made rice, chicken adobo, and lumpia.

"Mom! Not Filipino food again!" Tony said.

Tony wanted something new to eat.

"This is food from our culture, Tony," his mom said.

"But I want to eat something different," Tony said.

"What do you want to eat?" asks Mom.

"I want chicken nuggets!" said Tony. He licked his lips. He loved chicken nuggets.

Tony's mom looked at his sisters, who were eating the dinner she made. "Okay, Tony. Tomorrow you can eat chicken nuggets," she said.

Tony smiled. He could not wait until tomorrow!

The next day Tony ate his chicken nuggets with a big smile on his face. His sisters ate the soup and rice his mom made. They had big smiles on their faces, too.

I Like My Culture

Tony ate chicken nuggets the next day. And the next day. And the day after that! Tony ate chicken nuggets for four days. His mom made Filipino food for the rest of the family every day. His sisters loved the food from their culture.

Tony started to feel sad. He missed eating food with his family. He was getting tired of chicken nuggets. He missed his mom's food.

On Friday, Tony saw his mom putting chicken nuggets into the oven. Tony asked, "The chicken adobo and rice smells good. Can I have that tonight?"

Tony's mom looked at the chicken nuggets. "You don't want these, Tony?"

"No. I miss Filipino food. And I want to eat with my family."

Tony's mom smiled. "Of course you can," she said, giving him a hug. "And you are always part of the family, no matter what you eat."

I Like My Culture

Name _____

My Culture's Food

Tony likes to eat with his family. They sometimes eat rice and lumpia. They also eat chicken adobo. This is food from his Filipino culture.

Answer the items below.

1. Do you like to eat this food with your family? Circle **yes** or **no**.

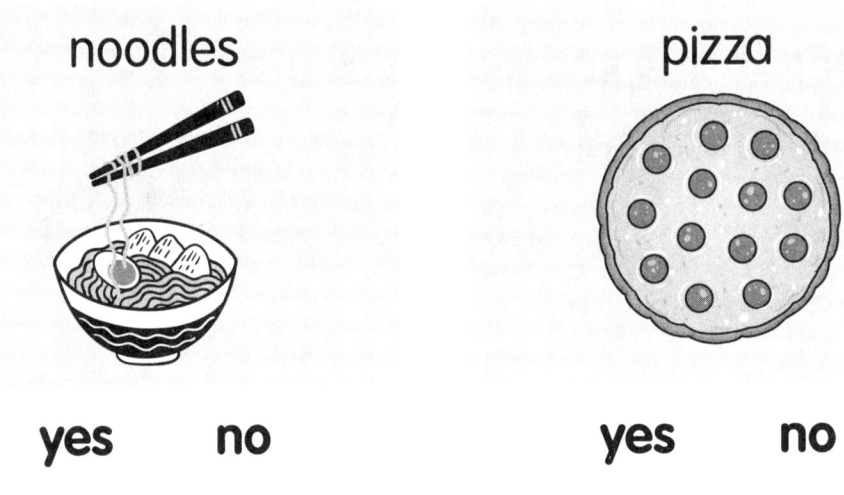

noodles   pizza

yes   no   yes   no

2. Draw a picture of a food you eat from your culture.

I Like My Culture

Name _____

Let's Talk About the Story

Tony learned that the food his mom cooks is not boring. It is food that makes him feel close to his family.

Think about these questions. Then talk with your classmates. You can tell them how you feel. You can listen to how they feel.

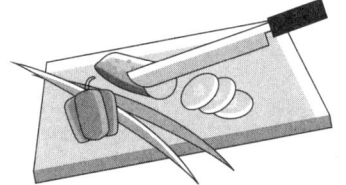

Have you ever felt like Tony? Tell what happened.

Does eating food you like make you feel happy?
Does eating food you do not like make you feel sad?

I Like My Culture

Name _____

Name _____

Let's Make Dinner! Partner Activity

Sometimes people in the same family like to eat different things. Some people like to eat food from their culture. Some people like to eat different food.

1. Together with your partner, make dinner for a family. Read about what each person wants to eat for dinner.

2. Then cut out the food pictures on page 77 and glue them to the table to make the dinner.

3. Everyone in the family likes Filipino food, so include 2 Filipino foods.

 Dad likes to eat rice.

 Mom likes to eat vegetables.

 Sister likes to eat soup.

 Brother likes to eat chicken nuggets.

I Like My Culture

Name _____

Name _____

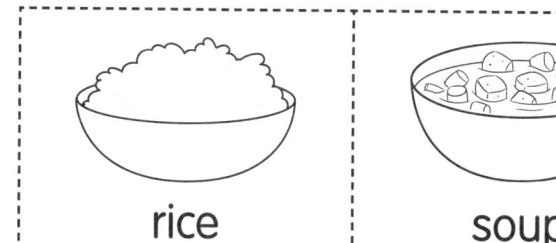

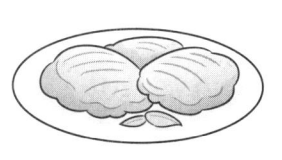

rice   soup   pizza   Filipino chicken

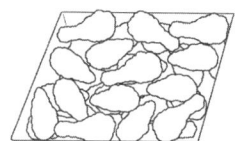
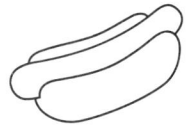

Filipino noodles   vegetables   chicken nuggets   hot dog

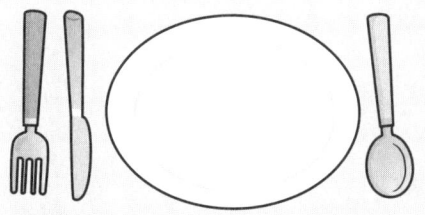

glue	glue	glue
glue	glue	glue

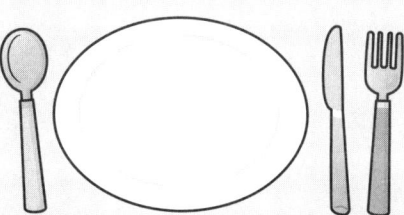
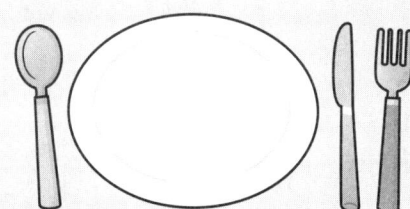

I Like My Culture

Choose Your Project— I Like My Culture

Tony's family is Filipino. At first, Tony does not know just how much he loves the food of his culture. Then he misses it!

What do you like about your culture? Choose a project that shows what you like about your family's culture.

1. Draw an **X** in the box next to the project you chose.

2. Give this paper to your teacher.

☐ **Paint a Picture**
Paint a picture that shows what you like about your culture.

☐ **Make a Video**
Make a video that shows something you like about your family's culture.

I Like My Culture—Painting

Paint a picture of something you like about your culture or your family life.

What You Need

- a large sheet of construction paper
- page 80
- paints
- a paintbrush
- crayons
- scissors
- glue or tape
- materials to decorate the border or outside of your painting, such as beads, colored tissue paper, pompoms, cotton balls, dry pasta, buttons, glitter, etc.

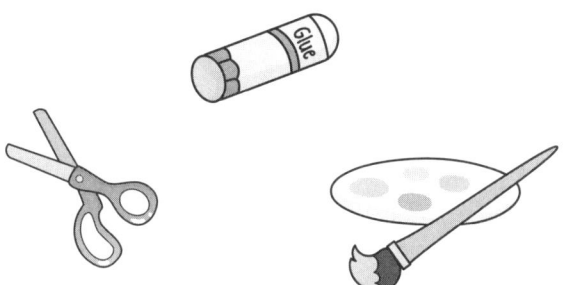

What You Do

1. Paint a picture. You can also choose to use the pictures on page 80 in your painting if you want. Color the pictures and cut them out. Then glue or tape them onto the construction paper with your painting.

2. Decorate the top, bottom, and sides of your painting.

3. Let your painting dry. Then show it to your friends.

I Like My Culture

Name _____

I Like My Culture—Video

Make a video that shows a part of your culture that you like.

What You Need

- a smartphone or camera
- page 82
- a pencil

What You Do

1. Think about something you really like about your family's culture or home life. What is something you want to show to other people on a video?

   Ideas for the video:
   - show a party or celebration
   - show a mealtime
   - show a dance
   - show music
   - show an activity your family does together

2. Write and draw on page 82 to plan your video.

3. Ask an adult to help you make the video.

4. After you make the video, watch it to make sure it looks good to you. Then show it to your friends.

What my video will show:

What I will say in my video:

Do the Right Thing

Friends Do the Right Thing

This unit is about how making choices that are kind, safe, and helpful can sometimes result in outcomes that are positive for everyone involved. Students will read about Kavya and Brenda, two friends who do not want to let the new girl in school play with them, but who eventually have a change of heart and choose to be kind. Students may have had experiences with making difficult choices, or they may learn some new ways to help them make choices. This unit will help students to stop and think before they act and to try to do the right thing. As you guide students through these topics, consider their varying world views as they share their experiences and make connections to their own lives.

The pages in this unit are reproducible. Reproduce the unit in its entirety or choose the pages that you wish to have your students do. A suggested teaching path is below.

1. **Read the Realistic Fiction Story (pages 84 and 85)**
   Distribute one copy of the text to each student. Have students read the text independently or read the text aloud as they follow along silently.

2. **I Can Do the Right Thing (page 86)**
   Distribute one copy of the page to each student. Guide students in completing the page independently.

3. **Let's Talk About the Story (page 87)**
   Distribute one copy of the page to each student. Facilitate a whole-group discussion or divide the class into small groups.

   Prepare for discussion:
   Guide students through reading each question. Give them time to think of their answers and to write them if they want to. Then facilitate a group discussion, encouraging students to share their thoughts.

4. **Stop and Think and Right or Wrong Partner Activities (pages 88 and 89)**
   Divide students into groups of two. Distribute one copy of each page to each group. Have each group work on the activity together.

5. **Choose Your Project—Choose the Right Thing (pages 90–94)**
   Distribute one copy of the project menu to each student. Explain to students that they will each choose a project to do. After students have chosen their project, collect the project menus. Reproduce and distribute the following project pages for each student based on the student's choice:
   - Pages 91 and 92 for Choose the Right Thing—Sign
   - Pages 93 and 94 for Choose the Right Thing—Book

   Decide whether or not students will share their finished projects with the class and instruct students accordingly.

Friends Do the Right Thing

Farah is at a new school. She wants to make friends. She asks if she can play with two girls in her class.

"Can I play with you?" Farah asks Brenda and Kavya.

"Yes," says Kavya.

"No," says Brenda.

Kavya asks Brenda, "Why can't she play with us?"

"I only want to have one friend, not two friends," Brenda says to Kavya. "I don't want to change our game."

Kavya feels sad for Farah. "Sorry, we don't want to play," says Kavya. Farah walked away. She was sad. She had no one to play with.

After school, Kavya walked home with her big brother, Clay. She told him about what happened.

She told him that she did not think that she and Brenda did the right thing. They should have let Farah play with them.

"I think you should tell Brenda how you feel," said Clay.

Do the Right Thing

"Mom and Dad always tell us to be kind to people, and what Brenda did was not kind."

The next day at school, Kavya sat next to Brenda at lunch. She gave Brenda one of her cookies. Kavya smiled. "Friends are kind to each other. You are kind to me, and I am kind to you. But I think we can be kind to a lot of people. Not just each other."

Later that day it was time to do art. Their teacher asked them to pick partners. Kavya and Brenda were always partners.

Brenda looked at Farah and saw that she did not have a partner. Brenda thought about what Kavya said at lunch. Then she walked over to Farah and said, "Sorry I did not let you play with us. I want to be your friend. Do you want to be partners with me and Kavya?"

Farah smiled and said "Yes!"

Kavya felt good inside. Her friend Brenda did the right thing. It felt good to be kind.

I Can Do the Right Thing

Your friend is sad. Look at the picture. Then draw a circle around the sentence that tells what you should do.

1.

   I should laugh at my friend.

   I should give my friend a hug.

2. Oh no! You knocked over your friend's block house. You did not mean to. But now your friend is sad.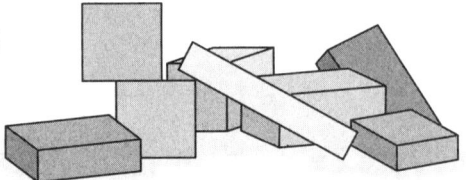

   Draw a picture to tell how you can help your friend.

Do the Right Thing Name _____

Let's Talk About the Story

Kavya and Brenda learned that doing the right thing means being kind or helpful to friends or family.

Think about these questions. Then talk with your classmates. You can tell them how you feel. You can listen to how they feel.

Do you think Kavya and Brenda did the right thing when they did not let Farah play with them?

How do you feel if a friend does not want to play with you?

Do the Right Thing

Name _____

Name _____

Stop and Think Partner Activity

Before you do something, stop and think. If it is **safe**, **kind**, or **helpful**, it might be the right thing to do.

Look at the pictures with your partner. Write **yes** or **no** to answer the questions together.

pushing

sharing toys

Is it safe?	
Is it kind?	

Is it kind?	
Is it helpful?	

caring

making a mess

Is it helpful?	
Is it kind?	

Is it kind?	
Is it helpful?	

Do the Right Thing

Name _____

Name _____

Right or Wrong Partner Activity

Cut out the pictures below. Talk with your partner about each picture. Then glue each picture under **right** or **wrong**.

 right    wrong

being mean

sliding down

walking up the slide

yelling

cleaning up

Choose Your Project—
Choose the Right Thing

Kavya and Brenda learn that they can choose to do the right or wrong thing. Doing the right thing means you are being safe, kind, or helpful.

Choose a project that shows people how to do the right thing. Show people why they should do the right thing.

1. Draw an **X** in the box next to the project you chose.
2. Give this paper to your teacher.

☐ **Make a Sign**
Draw, color, and write words to help people remember to do the right thing.

☐ **Make a Book**
Write words and draw a picture to show others how you do the right thing.

Do the Right Thing

Name _____

Choose the Right Thing—Sign

Make a sign to show and tell how your friends can stop, think, and do the right thing. Show them ways to be kind.

What You Need

- a sheet of construction paper or a piece of cardboard
- page 92
- markers or colored pencils
- scissors
- glue or tape

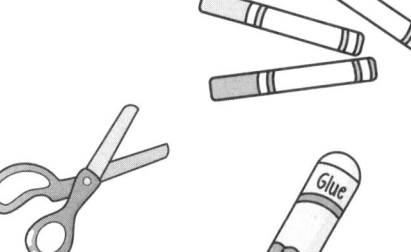

What You Do

1. Draw pictures of yourself doing the right thing by being safe, kind, or helpful. You can also use the words and pictures on page 92.

2. If you use the pictures and words on page 92, color them and cut them out. Then glue them to your sign.

3. Show your sign to your friends and family. Then hang it where you can see it.

right

DO THE RIGHT THING

wrong

think

kind

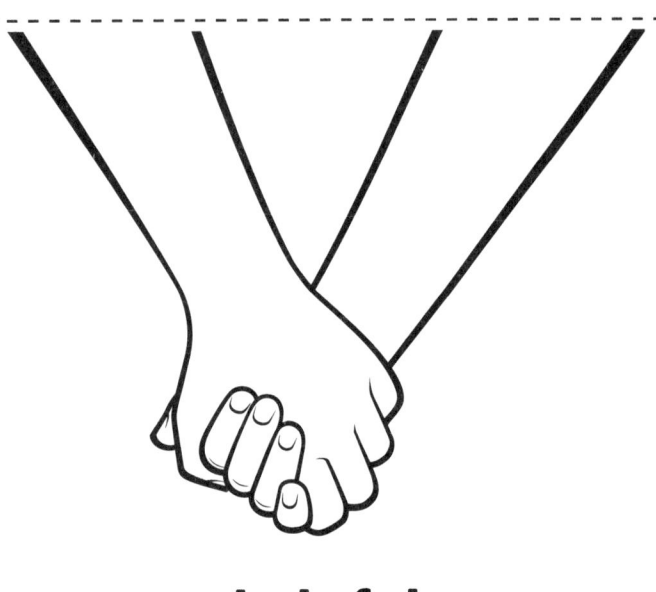
helpful

safe

92   Culturally Responsive Lessons and Activities • EMC 8261 • © Evan-Moor Corporation

Choose the Right Thing—Book

Write words and draw pictures to show your friends and family how you do the right thing.

What You Need

- page 94
- scissors
- a pencil
- crayons or markers

What You Do

1. Cut out page 94. Fold the paper in half. Then fold the paper in half again.

2. Write your name on the cover page. Then color the picture.

3. Write a word or a name to finish the sentence on each page.

4. Draw a picture on each page to show how you do the right thing.

5. Show your book to your friends and family.

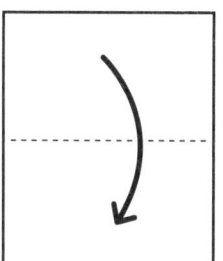
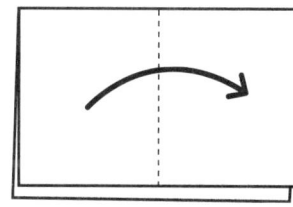

Do the Right Thing

I do the right thing when I help _____.

I do the right thing when I am kind to my friend named _____.

— fold —

— fold — | — fold —

DO THE RIGHT THING

by _____

I feel _____ when I do the right thing.

Do the Right Thing

Every Holiday Is Special

Three Holiday Parties

This unit is about celebrating different holidays and valuing what is special about each holiday. Students will read a story about a boy who has friends who celebrate different holidays. He goes to a Christmas party, a Kwanzaa party, and a Hanukkah party all in the same week and discovers that every holiday is special. Students may have their own experiences with friends and family members who celebrate different holidays, so they might connect to the story, or they may learn that every holiday is special to the people who celebrate it. As you guide students through these topics, consider their varying world views as they share their experiences and make connections to their own lives.

The pages in this unit are reproducible. Reproduce the unit in its entirety or choose the pages that you wish to have your students do. A suggested teaching path is below.

1. **Read the Realistic Fiction Story (pages 96 and 97)**
   Distribute one copy of the text to each student. Have students read the text independently or read the text aloud as they follow along silently.

2. **Your Holidays (page 98)**
   Distribute one copy of the page to each student. Guide students in completing the page independently.

3. **Let's Talk About the Story (page 99)**
   Distribute one copy of the page to each student. Facilitate a whole-group discussion or divide the class into small groups.

   Prepare for discussion:
   Guide students through reading each question. Give them time to think of their answers and to write them if they want to. Then facilitate a group discussion, encouraging students to share their thoughts.

4. **What a Holiday Means to You and Our Favorite Holidays Partner Activities (pages 100 and 101)**
   Divide students into groups of two. Distribute one copy of page 100 to each student. Distribute one copy of page 101 to each group. Have each group work on the activities together.

5. **Choose Your Project—Every Holiday Is Special (pages 102–106)**
   Distribute one copy of the project menu to each student. Explain to students that they will each choose a project to do. After students have chosen their project, collect the project menus. Reproduce and distribute the following project pages for each student based on the student's choice:

   - Pages 103 and 104 for Every Holiday Is Special—Picture Book
   - Pages 105 and 106 for Every Holiday Is Special—Finish the Story

Decide whether or not students will share their finished projects with the class and instruct students accordingly.

Every Holiday Is Special

Three Holiday Parties

"Kaleb, dinner is ready, so wash your hands," said Dad.

Kaleb washed his hands and sat at the table. The soup smelled good. "Hey Dad, can I go to Luna's Christmas party tomorrow?" asked Kaleb.

"Yes, I think so, but you are going to Kami's Kwanzaa party the next day. Will that be too much for you?" asked Dad.

"No. You know I love food and parties," Kaleb said with a smile. "Besides, it is winter break, so I don't have school."

Kaleb went to Luna's Christmas party on Monday. He saw his friend David there.

"Hey, Kaleb," said David, "my family is inviting a few people over for a Hanukkah party on Thursday. It is going to be a lot of fun! Can you come?"

"I think so! I have to ask my dad. I will let you know," said Kaleb.

Later that week, on Friday, Kaleb went to his mom's for dinner. They were having pizza, Kaleb's favorite.

Every Holiday Is Special

Name _____

"So, I heard that you went to three holiday parties this week," said his mom. "Wow! That must have been fun!"

"It was! And every party was different," said Kaleb.

"Tell me about them," said Mom.

"Well, Luna's family had a Christmas party," said Kaleb, "so we painted ornaments for the tree and ate Christmas cookies. Kami's family invited people over for Kwanzaa, so we made crafts to give to each other. I tried gumbo, and it was good! And David's family invited people for Hanukkah, so we played a game called dreidel and ate chocolates called gelt."

"Kaleb, those parties sound great," said Mom. "I am happy that you were able to go to all three of them!"

"Me too," said Kaleb. "I learned that every holiday is special. And even though every party was for a different holiday, there was one thing that was the same about all of them."

"What's that?" asked Mom.

"They all had friends, family, and food! Three of my favorite things!" laughed Kaleb.

Every Holiday Is Special   Name _____

Your Holidays

Kaleb's friends celebrated different holidays. Kaleb found out that every holiday is special.

Answer the items below.

1. Does your family celebrate a holiday during the winter or another time of year? Draw and write to tell about it.

2. Write or draw what you know or what you want to know about these winter holidays.

Kwanzaa

Every Holiday Is Special Name _____

Let's Talk About the Story

Luna, Kami, and David all celebrate different holidays in December. Some of the ways they celebrate are different, and some are the same.

Think about these questions. Then talk with your classmates. You can tell them what you think. You can listen to what they think.

How were the holiday parties the same? How were they different?

What makes a holiday special to you?

Every Holiday Is Special　　　　　Name _____

What a Holiday Means to You Partner Activity

People celebrate different holidays. They do different things to celebrate.

1. Write a ✔ in the boxes to show what a holiday means to you.

2. Write and draw two more things that a holiday means to you.

3. Give this paper to your partner. Tell your partner why you chose the things you did.

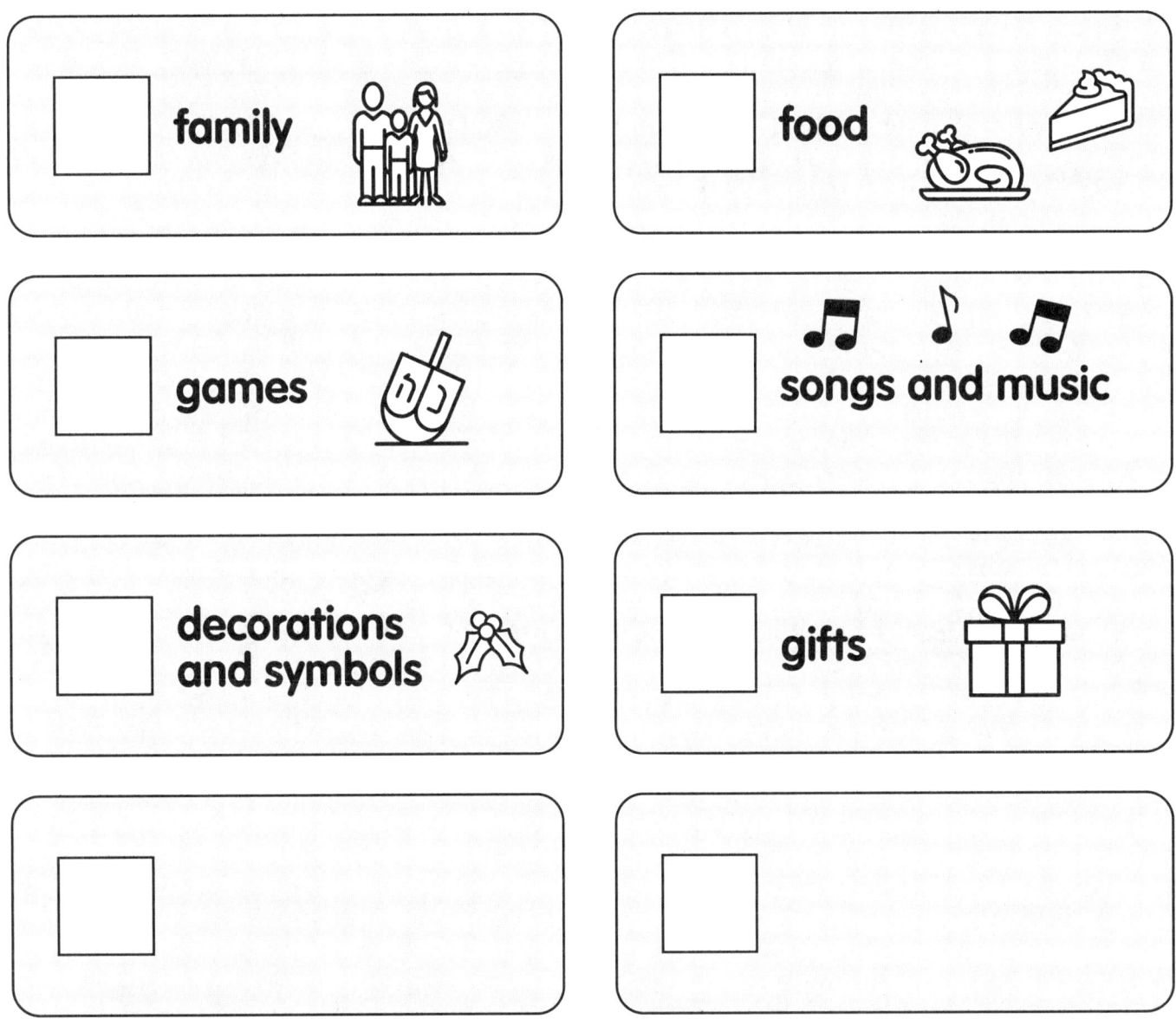

Every Holiday Is Special

Our Favorite Holidays Partner Activity

Draw a picture of your favorite holiday. Then write about it. Tell why it is special to you. Then give the page to your partner.

My favorite holiday is _____.

It is special because _____
_____.

My favorite holiday is _____.

It is special because _____
_____.

Every Holiday Is Special

Name _____

Choose Your Project—
Every Holiday Is Special

Some people celebrate Christmas. Some people celebrate Hanukkah. Some people celebrate Kwanzaa. Some people celebrate other holidays, too. Every holiday is special to the people who are celebrating it.

Think about holidays that are special to you. Choose a project to show or tell about holidays you like.

1. Draw an **X** in the box next to the project you chose.

2. Give this paper to your teacher.

☐ **Make a Picture Book**
Draw pictures to show your three favorite holidays.

☐ **Finish the Story**
Write words to finish the story about a holiday party.

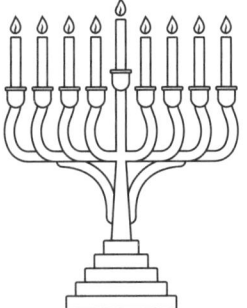

Every Holiday Is Special— Picture Book

Draw pictures that show what you like about your 3 favorite holidays.

What You Need

- 2 sheets of white or light-colored construction paper
- page 104
- crayons or markers
- other decorations, such as glitter, fabric, or popcorn
- a stapler
- scissors
- glue

What You Do

1. Choose your 3 favorite holidays to draw pictures of in your book. Think of what you like about each holiday.

2. Fold each sheet of construction paper in half. Put one folded paper inside the other to make a book.

3. Staple the left side on the top, middle, and bottom to make the sheets of paper open like a book.

4. On the inside pages of the book, draw pictures of your 3 favorite holidays.

5. Write your name on page 104. Color and cut out the page. Then glue it to the front cover of your book.

6. Decorate the front cover of your book.

Every Holiday Is Special

Every Holiday Is Special—Finish the Story

Write words to finish the story about a holiday party.

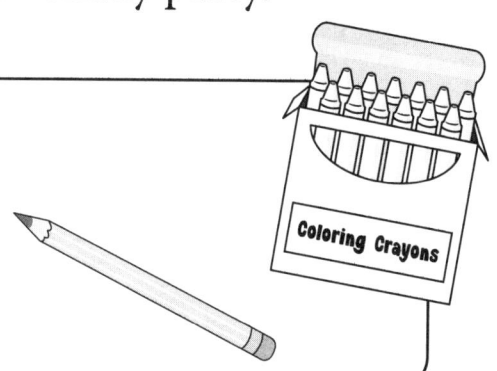

What You Need

- page 106
- a pencil
- crayons or markers

What You Do

1. Look at page 106. Read the story with the missing words.
2. Think about which holiday you will write about.
3. Write words to finish the sentences.
4. Draw pictures to tell about your story.
5. Read your story to someone.

A Special Holiday Party

_____ is having a party to celebrate
name of child

_____.
name of holiday

There will be _____ people at the party.
number of people

They will eat _____ and _____.
food   food

They will play _____ and sing
game

_____.
name of song

This holiday is special to the people at the party because
_____
_____
_____.

Classroom Community

Classroom Community

This unit is about helping the students in your classroom understand that together, they form a community. The activities in this unit can help students think about cooperation, empathy, friendship, and diversity. Through these activities, students may reach the understanding that it can feel good to be part of a group, and a world, with diversity. The purpose of this unit is to empower students to make good choices in the classroom by understanding empathy, teamwork, and the beauty in diversity.

The pages in this unit are reproducible. Reproduce the unit in its entirety or choose the pages that you wish to have your students do.

1. **Classroom Rules (page 108)**
   Distribute one copy of the page to each student.

2. **Guess Who! (pages 109 and 110)**
   Divide students into groups of two. Distribute one copy of page 109 to each group. Distribute one copy of page 110 to each student. Provide students with the materials needed for this activity. Collect all pages. With the whole group, have the students guess which classmate each page is about.

3. **How Do They Feel? (page 111)**
   Distribute one copy of the page to each student.

4. **Pass the Hula-Hoop (page 112)**
   Divide students into groups of 4 or more to play the game. Distribute one copy of the page to each group and explain to students how to play the game. Provide a Hula-Hoop to each group. If students can work together as a team to complete the challenge, add one more Hula-Hoop to each circle. Loop one Hula-Hoop on one student's left arm and right arm. Then have the class pass the Hula-Hoops in opposite directions.

5. **Sharing (page 113)**
   Distribute one copy of the page to each student.

6. **Good Choices in the Classroom (page 114)**
   Distribute one copy of the page to each student.

7. **Balloon Game (page 115)**
   Divide students into groups of 2–4. Distribute one copy of the page to each group. Explain how to play the game to students. Provide 4 balloons to each group.

8. **Same and Different Handprints (page 116)**
   Distribute one copy of the page to each student. Provide students with the materials needed.

9. **Give Shout-outs! (pages 117 and 118)**
   Distribute one copy of each page to each student. Provide students with the materials needed.

Classroom Community

Classroom Rules

People in a community follow rules to keep everyone safe and happy. Circle the rules that you want in your classroom.

I can share.

I can make a mess.

I can be kind.

I can help.

I can take my friend's toy.

I can yell.

Classroom Community

Guess Who!

Every person is special. Get to know more about the people in your classroom by doing this activity.

What You Need

- a partner
- page 110
- markers or colored pencils

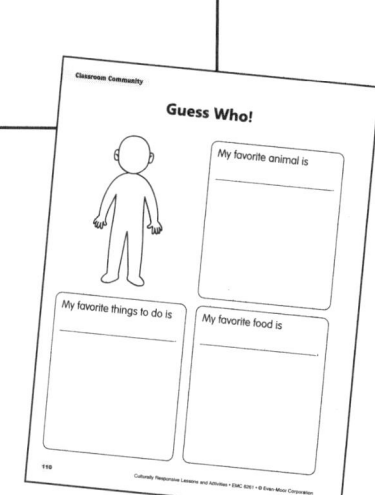

What You Do

1. Pick a partner.

2. Draw a picture of your partner on page 110.

3. Write words to finish the sentences that tell about your partner. Draw a picture to go with each sentence.

4. Give your paper to your teacher.

5. The teacher will hold up each page. Your class must guess which person the page tells about.

Classroom Community

Guess Who!

My favorite animal is
_____.

My favorite thing to do is
_____.

My favorite food is
_____.

Classroom Community   Name _____

How Do They Feel?

Everyone has feelings. You can sometimes know what a person is feeling by looking at his or her face and body.

Look at the pictures. Write a word and draw a face to show how the child feels.

 happy    angry    surprised    sad

1.

2.

3.

4.

Classroom Community

Pass the Hula-Hoop

People in a community work together to solve problems. Work as a team with your classmates to play this fun game.

What You Need

- 4 or more classmates
- 1 or 2 Hula-Hoops

What You Do

1. Hold hands with your classmates in a circle.

2. Loop one Hula-Hoop around one person's arm.

3. Try to pass the Hula-Hoop around the circle as fast as possible without letting go of anyone's hands.

Classroom Community

Name _____

Sharing

People in a community treat each other nicely. People in a community care for each other, too. Sharing shows you care.

Pretend your friend will not share a toy with you.

1. Finish the sentence to tell how you feel when a friend does not share with you.

   I feel _____ when my friend does not share with me.

2. What would you do if your friend did not share? Fill in the circles.

yell at your friend

tell your friend how you feel

play with a different toy

make a face at your friend

Classroom Community

Name _____

Good Choices in the Classroom

The choices you make can help you and the people in your classroom community.

Look at the pictures. Color 👍 if it is a good choice.
Color 👎 if it is not a good choice.

1.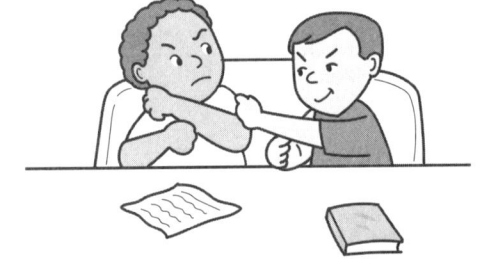

   fighting

2.

   asking for help

3.

   cleaning up

4.

   ripping or breaking things

Classroom Community

Balloon Game

Working together with other people can make things easier. In this game, you will try to keep the balloons in the air by yourself. Next, you will work with your classmates to keep the balloons in the air. Then you will see if working together or by yourself is easier.

What You Need

- groups of 2–4 people
- 4 balloons for each group

What You Do

1. Choose which person in the group will play first.

2. The first player must push all the balloons in the air, then keep tapping them to keep them all in the air as long as possible. If a balloon falls on the ground, the player is out, and it is the next player's turn.

3. Repeat the game so each player in the group has a turn to play alone.

4. After every person has a turn, all players in the group will play at the same time. Work together to keep the balloons in the air.

5. When the game is over, talk with your group about if it was easier to play when you worked alone or as a team.

Classroom Community

Same and Different Handprints

All people are different in some ways and the same in some ways. Look at your handprints and your classmates' handprints to see how they are the same and different.

What You Need

- paints
- light-colored construction paper
- a marker
- a paper plate
- a place to hang or lay out all of the handprints

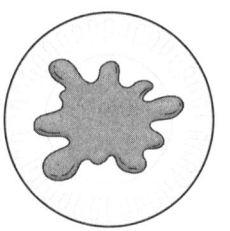

What You Do

1. Use the marker to write your name on the construction paper.

2. Pour paint onto the paper plate.

3. Dip each hand into the paint. Then press your hands onto the construction paper.

4. Let the paint dry. Then put your handprints with your classmates' handprints.

5. Look at all of the handprints with your classmates. Talk about how they are the same. Then talk about how they are different.

Classroom Community

Name _____

Give Shout-outs!

A shout-out is something you say to tell someone **thank you** or **good job**. When you give a shout-out, you can make people feel happy. Give shout-outs to your classmates.

What You Need

- page 118
- scissors
- crayons or markers

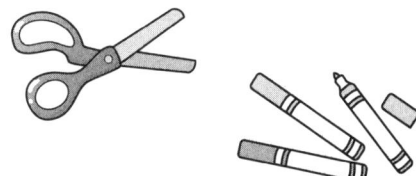

What You Do

1. Color and cut out each shape on page 118.

2. Read the words on the shapes. Think of people in your class you want to give shout-outs to.

3. Draw a picture on the back of the shapes to show why you are giving your classmate a shout-out.

4. Give each shout-out to the person you made it for.

Classroom Community

You are a **great friend!**

Thank you!

You make me **happy!**

You did it!

Culture and Family

Culture and Family

This unit helps students learn more about their own culture and other people's cultures. Explain to students that culture is the way a group of people live their lives. Culture includes the food people eat, what they wear, the language they speak, and the things they believe are important. Through these activities, students will learn more about the world around them. The purpose of this unit is to encourage students to accept and celebrate differences.

The pages in this unit are reproducible. Reproduce the unit in its entirety or choose the pages that you wish to have your students do.

1. **Culture Words (page 120)**

   Distribute one copy of the page to each student. This page is intended to be used as a reference for students.

2. **My Family (page 121)**

   Distribute one copy of the page to each student.

3. **Same and Different Partner Activity (page 122)**

   Divide students into groups of two. Distribute one copy of the page to each group.

4. **How I Say Hello (page 123)**

   Distribute one copy of the page to each student.

5. **Dinner Time (page 124)**

   Distribute one copy of the page to each student.

6. **My Favorite Game (pages 125 and 126)**

   Distribute one copy of each page to each student. Encourage students to finish the project at home by recording themselves playing their favorite game.

7. **Celebrations (page 127)**

   Distribute one copy of the page to each student. Explain to students that a celebration is a special gathering that honors a person, day, or event. A tradition is a belief or something that you do from time to time.

8. **Special Day Clothes (pages 128 and 129)**

   Distribute one copy of each page to each student. Provide students with the materials needed for this activity and with space to move around safely.

9. **Music Around the World (page 130)**

   Make a playlist that showcases music from around the world. Include popular songs that are age-appropriate from your country. Distribute one copy of the page to each student and provide a space for students to move around safely.

Culture Words

Words can tell about a person's **culture**. Read about culture.

What Is Culture?

Culture is many things. Culture is food, clothes, music, manners, and holidays. Culture is how we behave. Culture helps us learn about people from the past. It is what people have done for years. Culture can make people feel at home.

Every country or place has a different culture. Each family has its own culture, too.

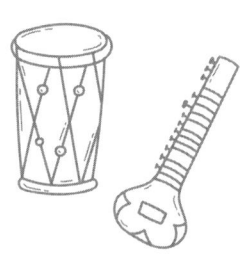

What is your family's culture? Read the words. In the squares, draw an **X** by the words that tell what your family likes or does.

| snow | cooking | horses | jokes | dancing |

| picnics | TV | music | sports | animals |

Culture and Family

Name _____

My Family

All families are different. A family can include parents, brothers and sisters, grandparents, pets, and friends, too. We learn how to behave from our families.

Draw a picture of your family. Then finish the sentences to tell more about your family.

Write a number to finish the sentence.

1. My family has _____ people.

2. My family has _____ pets.

Write a word or words to finish the sentence.

3. The language my family speaks at home is _____.

4. What I love to do most with my family is

_____

_____.

Culture and Family

Name _____

Name _____

Same and Different Partner Activity

All families are different. Families are the same in many ways, too.

Read the poem with a partner. Then write or draw pictures to show how your families are the same and different.

Families are big, and families are small,
Families are different, we love them all!
Families are people that care about you,
My family is special, and yours is, too!
—Unknown

Ways that our families are the **same**	Ways that our families are **different**

Culture and Family

Name _____

How I Say Hello

People from different cultures say hello in different ways. Color the pictures that show how you like to say hello.

1.
wave

2.
hug

3.
bow

4.
fist bump

Dinner Time

People from different cultures eat different foods.

Draw pictures to show what you like to eat and drink for dinner. Draw what things you use to eat your meals with, like a fork, a spoon, chopsticks, or your hands.

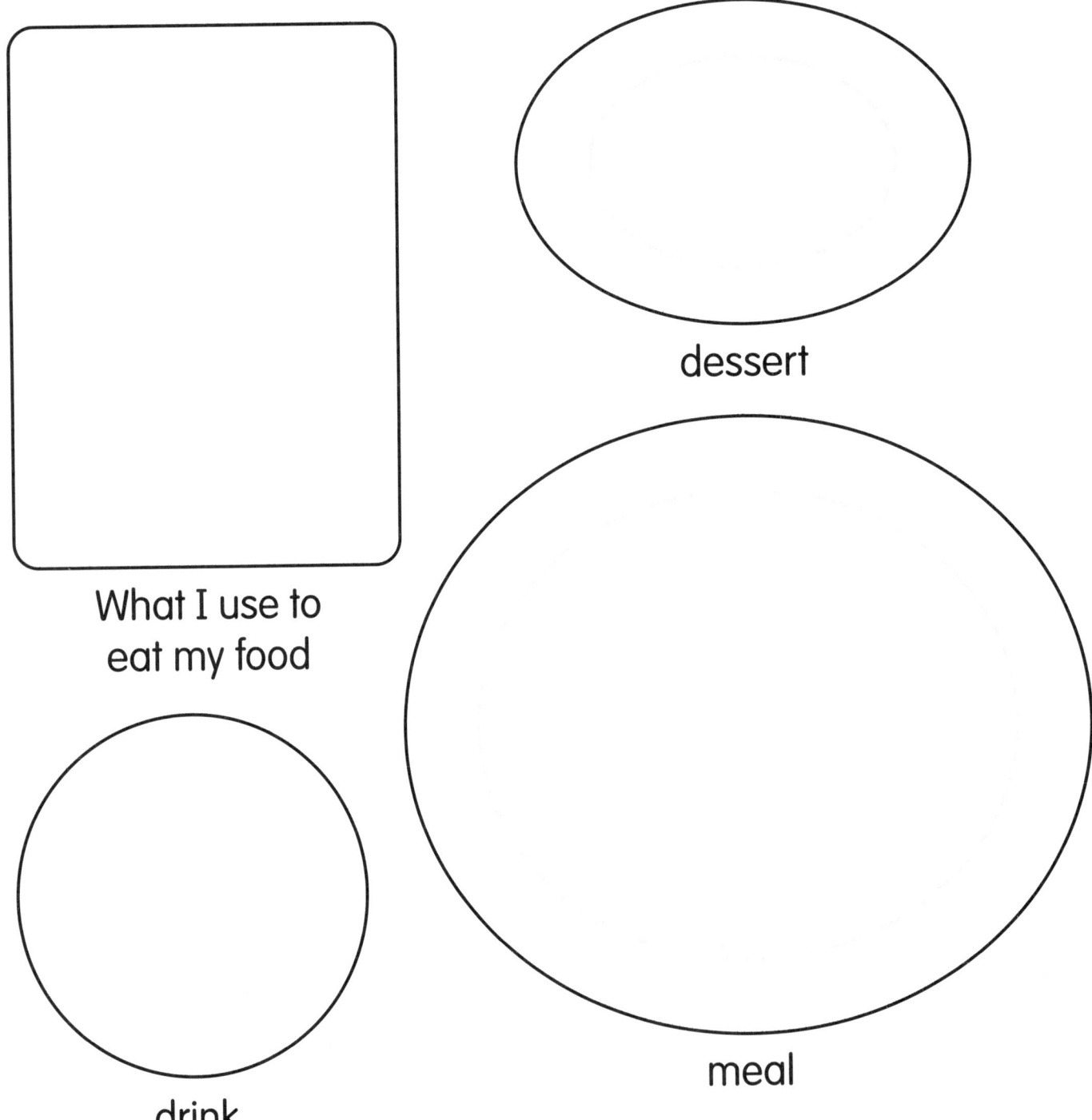

Culture and Family

Name _____

My Favorite Game

People around the world like to play games. Some people play games on holidays or for special celebrations.

What You Need

- page 126
- a pencil
- colored pencils or markers
- optional: a smartphone and the things you need to play your game

What You Do

1. Think about a game you like to play with your family or friends.

2. Write or draw on page 126 to tell about the game.

3. Optional: Ask a grown-up to make a video of you playing the game with your family or friends. Show your video or page 126 to a friend.

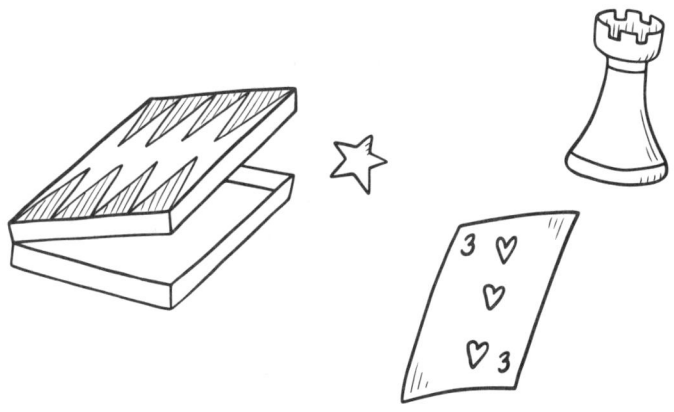

Culture and Family

Name _____

   # My Favorite Game

My favorite game to play is

What you need for the game

How you play the game

How many people can play

This is my favorite game because

Culture and Family

Name _____

Celebrations

People from different cultures have different celebrations.

Draw pictures or write words to tell more about a tradition or celebration in your family's culture.

My favorite family tradition or celebration is _____

_____.

Fun things we do	The foods we eat

Where we celebrate	This celebration is special to me because
	_____ _____ _____ _____.

© Evan-Moor Corporation • EMC 8261 • Culturally Responsive Lessons and Activities

Culture and Family

Name _____

Special Day Clothes

Some people wear special clothes on special days, like a birthday, wedding, or holiday. Show your classmates what you like to wear or what you have seen people wear on special days.

What You Need

- page 129
- scissors
- crayons or markers
- optional: buttons, beads, felt, glitter, construction paper, etc.

What You Do

1. Cut out the shape on page 129.

2. Use crayons, markers, or other materials to make your special day outfit.

3. Show your finished project to a classmate and tell about when you wear or see these special clothes.

128   Culturally Responsive Lessons and Activities • EMC 8261 • © Evan-Moor Corporation

Culture and Family

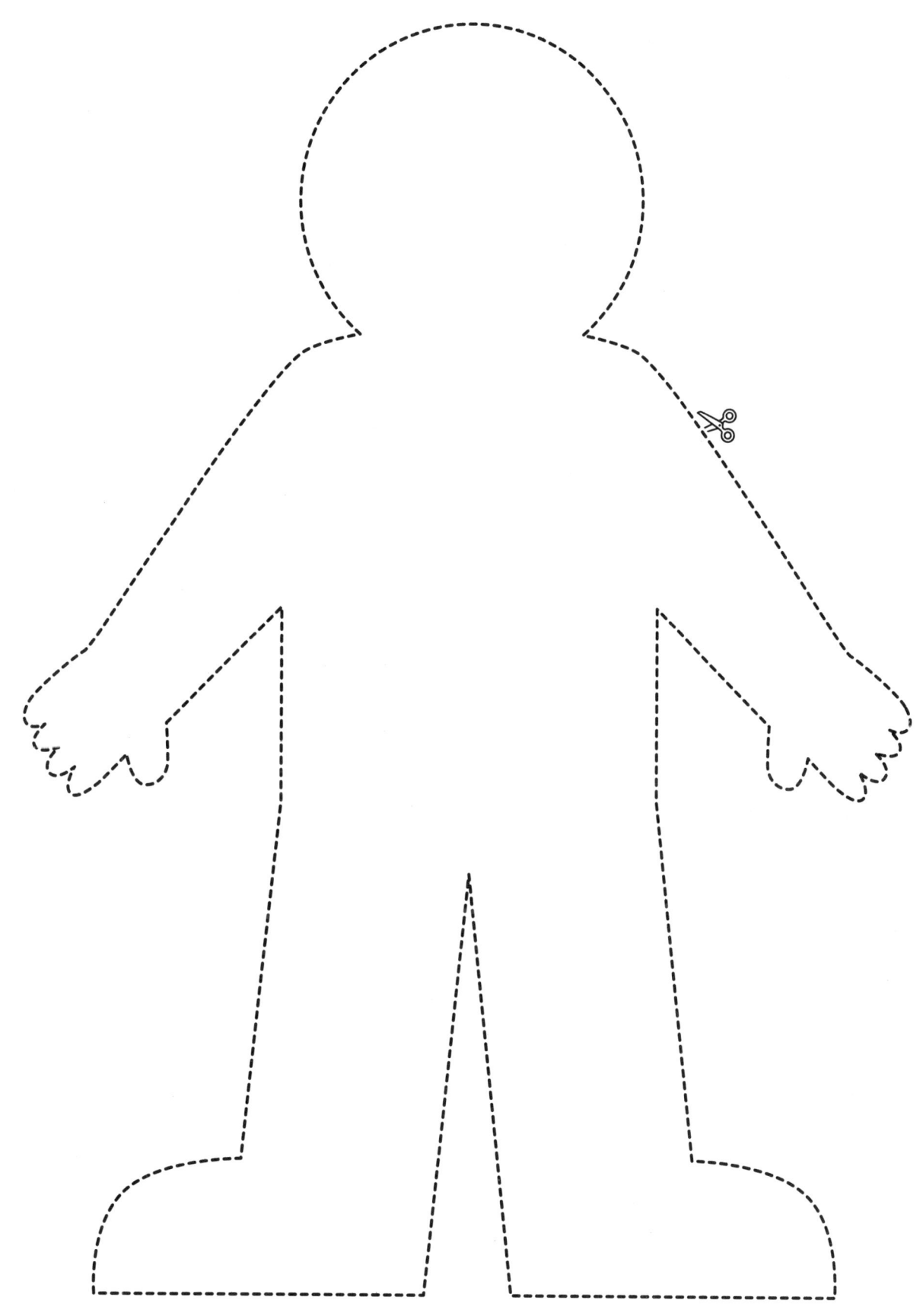

Culture and Family

Name _____

Music Around the World

People from different cultures listen to different kinds of music. Music sounds different in different places around the world. You can learn more about different cultures by listening to the words and instruments in a song.

What You Need

- music from around the world
- a speaker

What You Do

1. Find somewhere in the room where you have space to dance.

2. Your teacher will play a song.

3. Listen to the music and have fun dancing!

4. While you dance, think about how the music makes you feel. Listen to the words and the instruments you hear.

5. Talk to your friends about which songs you listen to in your home.

Classroom Quilt

Classroom Quilt

This unit provides resources for you and your students to make a quilt together. Each person will contribute an individual quilt square to the classroom quilt. The purpose of the quilt is for students to learn more about themselves and each other. It also helps you to learn more about each of your students. As you introduce this project to students, keep in mind that some students may be happy to share details about themselves, while others may not feel comfortable doing so. It is important to create a safe space for students to share without feeling judged or uncomfortable about who they are and where they come from. This is intended to be an inclusive experience that creates positive relationships and fosters understanding of each other.

1. **What Is a Quilt? (page 133)**
   Distribute one copy of this page to each student. This activity is intended to introduce quilts to students and show them what they look like. Explain to students that they will make a quilt square. Their quilt square will be put together with their classmates' squares to make one big class quilt. Explain to students that they can use their quilt square to tell about themselves. Explain that they can also learn about their classmates from the class quilt.

2. **About Me (page 134)**
   Distribute one copy of this page to each student. This activity will guide students to reflect about themselves and what they might want to share about themselves. Remind students that a family can include anyone they love, including pets, grandparents, and friends.

3. **My Favorite Places (page 135)**
   Distribute one copy of this page to each student. This activity will guide students to think about their favorite places they like to go with their friends and family, or even a make-believe place they visit in their dreams.

4. **Words on Quilts (page 136)**
   Distribute one copy of the page to each student. This activity helps students think about what words they want to include on their quilt square.

5. **Name Poem (pages 137 and 138)**
   Distribute one copy of each page to each student. This activity helps students think about how they feel about themselves and what they want others to know about them. Go over the examples at the bottom of page 137 and model a poem using your name. Encourage students to ask for help spelling any words.

6. **Quilt Shapes and Patterns (pages 139 and 140)**
   Distribute one copy of each page to each student. This activity helps students practice drawing shapes and patterns they might use on their quilt square. Tell students they can practice using shapes to make a picture. Provide students with glue and scissors to complete the activity.

7. **Quilt Colors (page 141)**

   Distribute one copy of the page to each student. Provide students with crayons, colored pencils, or markers. This activity helps students think about what words they want to include on their quilt square.

8. **Creating the Class Quilt (pages 142–144)**

   Practice Your Quilt Square (page 142)

   Distribute one copy of this page to each student. This page is intended to be the final draft page, which students can use to practice making their quilt square. Explain to students that they can use this page to draw what their final quilt square will look like. Tell students that they can look at the other pages they have finished for ideas on what to add to their quilt square.

   Quilt Square Directions and Quilt Square Page (pages 143 and 144)

   Provide students with the materials listed on page 143 below What You Need. Distribute one copy of pages 143 and 144 to each student. Guide students as they follow the steps below What You Do to make their individual quilt square for the class quilt.

   Putting the quilt squares together to make the class quilt

   Collect each student's quilt square. Then attach all of the pictures using a stapler or tape, punching holes and threading yarn or string, or using tacks on a bulletin board, corkboard, or tackboard. You may choose to have students help put the pictures together. After the individual squares are put together, decide where to place the class quilt so that it can be seen. Encourage students to look at the pictures and use them to try to learn about their classmates.

Classroom Quilt

Name _____

What Is a Quilt?

A quilt is a blanket that is made from small pieces of fabric put together. A quilt can have many different colors, shapes, and patterns. A quilt can have words on it, too.

Quilts are important because they tell more about the people who make them and the people the quilts are made for. The pictures, patterns, and words on quilts have special meanings. People use quilts to keep them warm. People use quilts as decoration. Some cultures give quilts to people on special days like a birthday, wedding, or graduation or to welcome a new baby.

Classroom Quilt

Name _____

About Me

A quilt can tell about the person who made it.
Draw a picture or write words in each shape to tell about yourself.

- my favorite thing to do
- my favorite book
- my favorite movie
- a picture of me
- my favorite animal
- my favorite food
- my family

Classroom Quilt

Name _____

My Favorite Places

A quilt can tell about the person who made it. The pictures and words on a quilt can show where you live, your favorite places to go, or somewhere you want to go.

Draw or write words in each box to tell about your favorite places.

My favorite place to go	A place I like to go with my family or friends
A place I would like to go one day	**A place I visit in my dreams**

Classroom Quilt

Words on Quilts

Some quilts have words that tell about a person. Some words on quilts tell what is important to the person.

1. Circle the words or groups of words you would like to see on a quilt.

   happy   funny   cool

   animal lover   Be Kind   I did it!

   love   Save the earth   brave

2. Write a word or group of words that you would like to have on a quilt.

   _____ _____ _____

Classroom Quilt Name _____

Name Poem

Some quilts have poems that tell people's names. Some poems tell what is important to people. Make a poem that tells about you.

What You Do

1. Write the first letter of your name in the first box on page 138.

2. Think about words that start with that letter that tell about you. You can write one word or a sentence. Look at the poems below.

3. Write the word or sentence on the line next to the letter in the box.

4. Write every letter in your name in each box, from top to bottom. Write words for every letter in your name. Every line of the poem should tell about you.

Examples:

A poem about Friends
F riends share toys
R eally nice
I like to play with them at the park
E very day we have fun
N ever make me sad
D ance with me
S ay kind words

A poem about a girl named **Tisha**
T alks a lot
I s a big sister
S ings songs
H appy and funny
A good friend

Classroom Quilt

Name _____

Classroom Quilt

Name _____

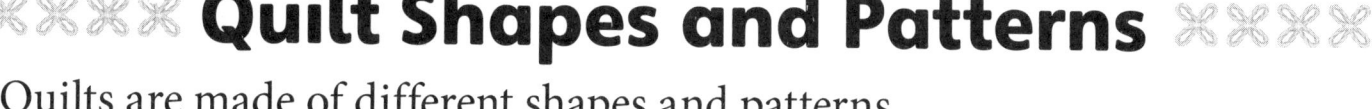

Quilt Shapes and Patterns

Quilts are made of different shapes and patterns. Some quilts use shapes to make a picture.

Draw shapes to finish the pattern.

1.

2.

Cut out the small shapes on page 140. Glue the shapes in the box below to make a pattern or picture.

© Evan-Moor Corporation • EMC 8261 • Culturally Responsive Lessons and Activities

Classroom Quilt

Quilt Shapes and Patterns

Classroom Quilt

Name _____

Quilt Colors

Quilts come in many different colors. Think about the colors you want to use on your quilt square.

1. Color the crayon with your favorite color.

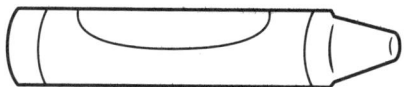

2. Color the crayon with your friend's favorite color.

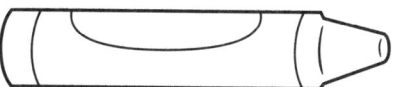

3. Color the shapes with colors you would like to use on your quilt square.

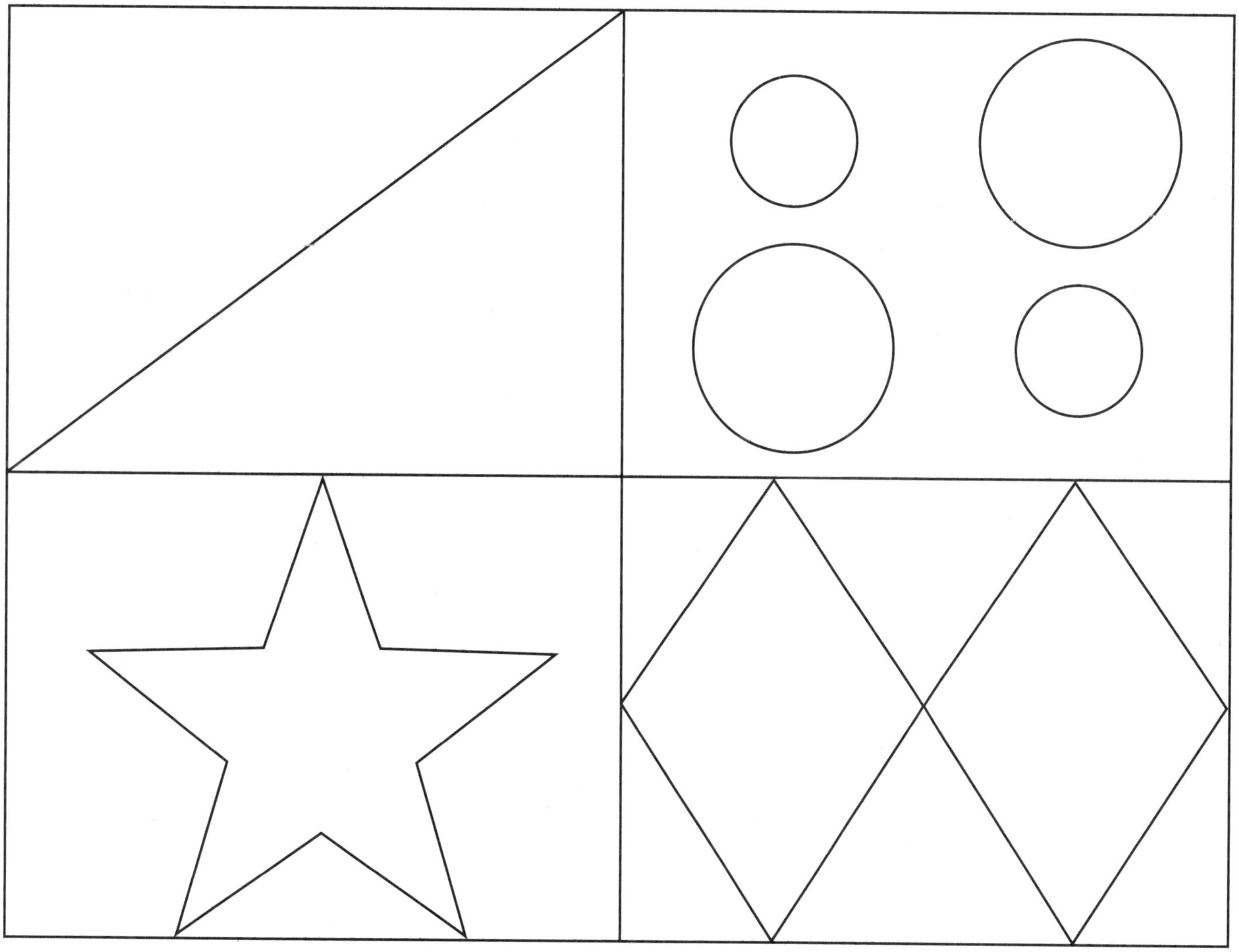

Classroom Quilt

Name _____

Practice Your Quilt Square

Draw to show what your quilt square will look like. Look at your answers from the other pages to get ideas about what you want to draw. Remember, your quilt can tell about you, your family, or your friends. It can have words, shapes, patterns, different colors, and pictures, too.

Classroom Quilt

Name _____

Quilt Square Directions

Make a quilt square to tell about yourself, your family, or your friends. Your picture will be part of a big class quilt.

What You Need

- pages 142 and 144
- colored pencils, crayons, or markers
- construction paper
- scissors
- glue or tape

What You Do

1. On page 142, practice making your quilt square. Draw what you want your quilt square to look like.

2. On page 144, you will make your quilt square. Use colored pencils, crayons, or markers to decorate the entire square.

3. Cut out the quilt square. Then glue it onto a piece of construction paper that is the same size.

4. Give your quilt square to your teacher.

Classroom Quilt